ty/Disclaimer of Warranty: While the publisher and author have used their best
ring this book, they make no representations or warranties with respect to the
mpleteness of the contents of this book and specifically disclaim any implied
merchantability or fitness for a particular purpose. No warranty may be created or
les representatives or written sales materials. The advice and strategies contained
t be suitable for your situation. You should consult with a professional where
either the publisher nor author shall be liable for any loss of profit or any other
mages, including but not limited to special, incidental, consequential, or other
ers should be aware that Internet Web sites offered as citations and/or sources for
ation may have changed or disappeared between the time this was written and
.

oks and products are available through most bookstores. To contact Jossey-Bass
ur Customer Care Department within the U.S. at 800-956-7739, outside the U.S.
986, or fax 317-572-4002.

hes in a variety of print and electronic formats and by print-on-demand. Some
uded with standard print versions of this book may not be included in e-books or in
hand. If this book refers to media such as a CD or DVD that is not included in the
purchased, you may download this material at http://booksupport.wiley.com. For
ation about Wiley products, visit www.wiley.com.

Congress Cataloging-in-Publication Data is Available:

18076828 (Hardcover)
18222676 (ePDF)
18236543 (ePub)

n by Wiley
e: Sunil S. Reddy

the United States of America

g 10 9 8 7 6 5 4 3 2 1

Buil
Scho

HOW TO CREATE THE

Chris Lehmann a

JB JOSSEY-B

A Wile

Contents

⁂

Chris: For Jakob and Theo—this book represents the best ideas I've had about what I hope school can be for you.

And for Kat, without whom I would never have done any of this.

Zac: For my parents, who taught me there are many wonderful ways to learn.

And for my Uncle David.

About the Authors

‡

Chris Lehmann is the founding principal of Science Leadership Academy, a progressive science and technology high school in Philadelphia, Pennsylvania. Considered a national ed-tech thought leader, Chris was named Outstanding Leader of the Year by the International Society of Technology in Education in 2013 and in 2014 was awarded the prestigious "Rising Star" McGraw Prize in Education.

Science Leadership Academy (SLA) is an inquiry-driven, project-based, one-to-one laptop school that is considered to be one of the pioneers of the School 2.0 movement nationally and internationally. A partnership with Philadelphia's Franklin Institute science museum, the school was recognized by *Ladies Home Journal* as one of the Ten Most Amazing Schools in the United States and has been recognized as an Apple Distinguished School. SLA has been highlighted on the PBS *NewsHour* as well as a broad range of publications such as *Edutopia*, *Education Week*, and the *Philadelphia Inquirer*.

In 2013, Chris spearheaded the drive to expand the SLA model to a second Philadelphia high school, SLA @ Beeber, and has signed on to start an additional Philadelphia middle school. He continues to work with schools and districts all over the world as a consultant. In 2013, he cofounded the non-profit

Inquiry Schools with Diana Laufenberg, where he serves as superintendent and chair of the board. The non-profit's mission is to expand SLA's inquiry-driven approach to more schools.

Among his many honors, Chris has been named by the White House as a Champion of Change for his work in education reform, heralded as one of Dell's #Inspire100 (one of the one hundred people changing the world using social media), named as one of the "30 Most Influential People in EdTech" by *Technology & Learning* magazine and received the Lindback Award for Excellence in Principal Leadership.

A popular speaker, Chris has spoken at conferences all over the world, including TEDxPhilly, TEDxNYED, the National Association of Secondary Schools Conference, SXSW, SXSWedu, the Building Learning Communities conference, the International Society of Technology in Education, and the International Conference on Technology and Education, and at the Central and Eastern European Schools Association Conference. Chris has written for such education publications as *Principal Leadership*, *Learning and Leading with Technology*, and the *School Library Journal*. He is coeditor of *What School Leaders Need to Know about Digital Technologies and Social Media* and the author of the education blog Practical Theory.

Chris received his B.A. in English literature from the University of Pennsylvania and his M.A. in English education from Teachers College, Columbia University. Chris returned to his native Philadelphia to start SLA after nine years as an English teacher, technology coordinator, girls' basketball coach and Ultimate Frisbee coach at the Beacon School in New York City, one of the leading urban public schools for technology integration. He is perhaps most proud to be father to Jakob and Theo. You can find Chris on Twitter at @chrislehmann.

Zac Chase loves learning and teaching. For eight years, Zac taught 8–12 grade students English—first in Sarasota, Florida, and then in Philadelphia at Science Leadership Academy (SLA). He is a National Fellow for the Institute for Democratic

Education in America. An original Freedom Writer Teacher, he's worked with teachers nationally through the Freedom Writers Foundation. Additionally, Zac works with teachers, schools, and school districts across the country as a consultant focused on reflective practice and the thoughtful combination of pedagogy and technology for teaching and learning. He has also worked internationally with schools and systems in Canada, Kenya, Malaysia, South Africa, and Pakistan to consider the intersection of learning, inquiry, reflective pedagogy, technology, and project-based learning. He is driven to investigate the role and importance of creativity, improvisation, and care in teaching and learning.

When not engaged directly in the work of helping schools and teachers improve their practice, Zac has his head down in a book, a blog, or the latest piece of education research.

Zac earned his M.E. in education policy and management from the Harvard Graduate School of Education, his master of teaching and learning in curriculum and instruction at NOVA Southeastern University, and his B.A. in English education from Illinois State University. A founding cochair of SLA's EduCon, Zac has presented at conferences around the country, including FETC, NCTE, IntegratED PDX and SF, and ISTE.

Zac has written for the *Journal of Adolescent and Adult Literacy* and the *Education Week* blog, and cowrote and edited the *New York Times* bestseller *Teaching Hope*. He blogs regularly at *autodidactic.com* and has taught and performed improvisational comedy since 1999. He works as an instructional technology coordinator in the St. Vrain Valley School District in Colorado, where he works with other district leaders as well as within schools to help leverage technology in support of learning and teaching. Through 2014–2015, Zac is on detail to the U.S. Department of Education Office of Educational Technology as a ConnectED Fellow. He is committed to creating deep, authentic, and engaging learning for all through the innovative use of resources. You can find him on Twitter at @MrChase.

About
Science Leadership Academy

How do we learn?
What can we create?
What does it mean to lead?

These three essential questions form the basis of instruction at the Science Leadership Academy (SLA), a Philadelphia high school opened in September 2006. SLA is built on the notion that inquiry is the very first step in the process of learning. Developed in partnership with The Franklin Institute and its commitment to inquiry-based science, SLA provides a vigorous, college-preparatory curriculum with a focus on science, technology, mathematics, and entrepreneurship. Students at SLA learn in a project-based environment where the core values of inquiry, research, collaboration, presentation, and reflection are emphasized in all classes.

The structure of SLA reflects its core values, with longer class periods to allow for more laboratory work in science classes and performance-based learning in all classes. In addition, students in the upper grades have more flexible schedules to allow for opportunities for dual enrollment programs with area universities and career development internships in laboratory and business settings, as well as with The Franklin Institute.

At SLA, learning is not just something that happens from 8:30 A.M. to 3:00 P.M., but a continuous process that expands beyond the four walls of the classroom into every facet of our lives.

Acknowledgments

⛬

The book exists because of the incredible spirit, joy, and hard work of everyone at the Science Leadership Academy—students, teachers, parents, and partners. The book also would never have happened without our friend and colleague Diana Laufenberg. She puts up with us both, and her friendship and counsel make us both better, and many of the ideas expressed in this book were workshopped with Diana. We probably need to apologize to her for all the stress this book caused her, just because she's our friend.

The book is peppered with references to friends and mentors we've known and collaborated with over the years, whose ideas and passion have informed our ideas and made us better teachers—folks like Mike Thayer, Chris Johnson, Jose Vilson, Audrey Watters, Tom Sobol, Bud Hunt, Will Richardson, David Warlick, Gary Stager, Sylvia Martinez, Jaime Casap, Marge Neff, Shelly Pavel, Janet Samuels, Melinda Anderson, Ira Socol, Pam Moran, John Spencer, David Jakes, Christian Long, Trung Le, Marilyn Perez, Simon Hauger, Lisa and Michael Clapper, Darlene Porter, Elyse Eidman-Aadahl, Paul Oh, Christina Cantrill, Dean Shareski, Dan Meyer, Stephen Stoll, and Ruth Lacey.

This book owes an incredible debt to the most patient editor in the world, Kate Bradford, and all the folks at Jossey-Bass Wiley who were incredibly patient with two very slow writers. Finally, thank you to our families who have put up with us through all the drafts. For Chris, that means a special thank-you to my incredible wife, Kat Stein, who probably hopes I never write another book ever again.

These pages also owe their existence to the students, teachers, and families of SLA. The work and learning they do together each day and through the years shows that these ideas are more than theories. They live and breathe these ideas as practices to be refined and reflected on toward building a better future and society.

Finally, thank you to those teachers in our lives throughout our years as students. To those who took the time to know us, to engage our curiosities, and to help us discover our worlds and the world at large: we stand on your shoulders and do what we can in hope of honoring your work.

Foreword

I t's an unusual high school that attracts teachers from across the country to work there. When the first SLA opened in 2006, I read along from my home in Flagstaff, Arizona, as Chris told the story of turning a Philadelphia office space into a school. The next year, when Zac left students he cherished in Florida to join the SLA faculty, I too thought about what it might mean to leave a place I loved to also walk that path.

While adventurous, I am still a Midwesterner at heart. Instead of just taking the leap, I dipped my toe in the water by attending the first-ever EduCon in January 2008. It was there that I first met Zac and Chris in person. The conference was intimate and thought-provoking, and as I headed home to Arizona I already had an inkling of what would happen next. By April, Chris offered me a position teaching kids history for the next year.

Joining the staff of Science Leadership Academy was like coming in from the cold for a little while. The environment for learning was superb, the teachers were and continue to be the most densely talented teaching staff, and there was still so much to vision and create as the school grew. Our days were spent minimizing the administrivia that can overwhelm the job and focusing on how to craft meaningful educational experiences, how to support the students and ourselves appropriately, and how to build the systems that would foster this environment. It was a heavy lift for all of us, but so worth the effort.

The school continues to be a magnet for people who feel that something has been missing from education, and teachers continue to pack up in other states to take jobs there. This book is the record of that work, the result of thousands of hours of verbal banter, arguments, jokes, heartfelt confessions, and frustrations, all of which breathe life into the school we all needed—students, parents, and staff alike.

During my four years there, I spent countless hours with Zac and Chris taking care of the administration and long-term planning for the school. Our work flow was definitely unusual. We spent (too) many late nights working around Chris's desk, cycling between watching *West Wing* clips on YouTube, sharing thought-provoking blog posts, quoting pithy tweets, being full-on ridiculous, and cranking out the work. I could tell you that we were efficient, but I'd be lying. Effective, yes, but efficient, no. Though the two of them may tell you that I was the "least fun" one, always trying to keep us on task, I stretched myself greatly while I was there with them. The farm kid born of efficiency had to stop and question not just whether the work was getting done, but whether our work honored the people we were working and learning with along the way. We were the model of distracted productivity, and it was grand.

Building School 2.0 is born of that distracted productivity, a blend of humanity and scholarly inquiry that fuels the daily dialogue at SLA. When we had a particularly challenging stretch, we truly would search to find the value of each school day. When we started taking ourselves a little too seriously, we reminded each other that humility matters and to not become ego-invested in our work. On those really amazing days when the teaching and learning flowed ever so smoothly, we reveled in how lucky we were to be teachers. And on almost a daily basis, we would be silly—and I mean really silly, the kind that leaves you teary-eyed and with sore abs. This book captures so much of what we cherish in that school environment, so much of what we are all still working to sustain at SLA and create in new learning environments.

Building School 2.0 is not a checklist of measurables or quantifiable data. The ninety-five "theses" here are the conversations to have with your friends over dinner, questions you can explore with your colleagues throughout the year, challenges to construct more modern and humane spaces for our most cherished resource: our students. When pondering the idea of School 2.0, stop arguing about the tests and the standards and the apps. Start considering that within this book are the beginnings of a dialogue that can change the way you create learning spaces for all the people at your schools. A dialogue that needs to be as unique and varied as the educational spaces that inhabit our world.

Chris and Zac have taken painstaking care to craft for us a window into a school committed to a set of classic ideals powered by modern tools, a place willing to critically question its own best ideas. While the three of us no longer work in the same space, reading this book was like coming in from the cold again. This is what it was like to sit in that office for four years while bantering, celebrating, crying, laughing, debating, and working. I miss it terribly, but this book takes me to a timeless place where that ethos can live and inspire more learning communities.

Diana Laufenberg

School Should Mirror the World as We Believe It Could Be

This book is borne of a spirit of hope that we can build healthier, more relevant, more caring schools that, in turn and in time, will help to build a healthier world.

According to Wolfram Alpha, there are fifty-nine million K–12 students in the United States.[1] That's fifty-nine million families' dreams, fifty-nine million young people whose lives are still loaded with potential, fifty-nine million young people whose stories have yet to be written, fifty-nine million students who deserve to be encouraged to believe, "You can," before having someone tell them, "You can't." For that matter, the over three million teachers[2] all over this country also deserve someone to tell them "You can," before having someone tell them, "You can't."

And yet, so much of what happens in school happens because we believe that we must prepare children for the world as it used to exist. Never mind that we have no idea what the world will look like for kids in kindergarten right now—and we might not even know what it will look like for the kids in ninth grade—we continue to replicate the factory-age structures and compliance-based codes of conduct that have governed school for decades because it "feels like school" to parents and politicians and school administrators all over the world.

Worse, in the twenty-first century the massive technological changes that have vastly changed our society have had little effect on our schools; in too many places, the technology is merely being used as the next, best filmstrip, or worse, a better way to quiz and test our students, rather than as a way to open up our classroom windows and doors so that students can learn what they need to, create what they want, and expand the reach of their ideas to almost limitless bounds.

In 1518, Martin Luther nailed ninety-five theses to the door of the church. He envisioned a world where the church did not act as a go-between—and in his mind, a barrier—between God and man. We need to understand now that school does not need to be a go-between—and, too often, it is a barrier—between students and learning. We can remake school so that students can feel more directly empowered to learn deeply alongside teachers who share a vision of the sense of joy that learning can unlock.

For our ninety-five theses, we ask you to suspend your disbelief that schools can be better than they are now. In fact, we ask you to suspend your disbelief that the world can be a better place. Each thesis in the text could lead to more questions, deeper discussion, more research, and, we hope, positive action. It is our hope that, individually, each thesis could help students and parents and educators to examine specific practices in their schools as they exist, and taken collectively, they can help communities create a new vision of school, built on the best of what has come before us, steeped in the traditions of progressive educators of the past hundred years, but with an eye toward a future we cannot fully imagine.

From Theory to Practice

- To prime your thinking as you move through the text, pause and take a moment to describe what you think school should be doing, what its role is in a modern world, and what success looks like. Let this thinking be a signpost as you explore this book.

- Start a conversation. As important as it is to think deeply about your own vision of what school can and should be, this book is designed as a conversation starter as well. As a thesis strikes you as relevant to your own place of learning and teaching, consider how you might use it to begin a larger conversation. Could you get time in a faculty meeting or a Parent-Teacher Association meeting, use it to inspire discussion as you have coffee with a colleague, or track key quotations and share them with a Listserv? Be on the lookout and be mindful. The more stories we share, the deeper our thinking will become.

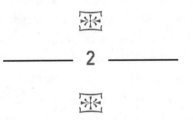

We Must End Educational Colonialism

Science Leadership Academy (SLA) was started by a group of educators with the idea that it would be the kind of school we would want our own children (real or theoretical) to attend. Our belief in an inquiry-driven, project-based, technology-rich approach to learning was not just for "other people's children," but for our own as well.

It is important to say this because there are a lot of powerful people right now who are advocating for a pedagogy in our publicly funded schools that they don't find good enough for their own children.[3] Some of these powerful people are even running networks of schools that have a pedagogical approach that is directly counter to the educational approach of the institutions they pay for their own children to attend. Moreover, these same powerful people tend to get upset when asked about the disconnect, saying that that question is off limits.

We don't think it is.

We should ask why people of power advocate for one thing for their own children and something else for other people's children, especially when those other children come from a lower rung on the socioeconomic scale or when those children come from traditionally disenfranchised segments of our society. It is, in fact, a very dangerous thing not to question.

Because we've done this before in America and around the world. Whether it was the United States government forcing Native Americans into boarding schools, which decimated families and societies in the name of assimilation, or any of the many global examples of destruction as explorers claimed "new worlds," history is rife with examples of disenfranchisement through systematic cultural colonization—each ending tragically.

For us, when you ensure that your own child has an arts-enriched, small-classroom-sized, deeply humanistic education and you advocate that those families who have fewer economic resources than you have should have to sit straight in their chairs and do what they are told while doubling and tripling up on rote memorization and test prep, you are guilty of educational colonialism.

And it's time we start calling that what it is.

The ideas in this book represent our best thoughts on education for all children, not just some children. If we are to truly engage in modern pedagogical education reform, it must be a movement of the cities and the suburbs, of public and private and charter schools, and for children of all colors and classes. To do anything else is to ignore the elephant in the room—that we are rapidly moving further and further into a bifurcated system in this country where the education rich children get is vastly different from the education poor children get.

We—all of us—must be committed to ensuring that the income of a child's parents or the color of a child's skin does not prevent the child from engaging in a profoundly humanistic, deeply empowering modern education. And if we allow those in power to advocate for a brand of education for other people's children that they would never allow for their own children, we will only perpetuate the worst abuses of our history.

From Theory to Practice

- Start the conversation. The best way to allow educational colonialism to persist is to remain silent about its presence. The best way to fight it is to start conversations across classrooms, schools, and districts that share our practices, our learnings, and our resources. Seek out colleagues in online and physical spaces that may feel foreign to you, and begin a conversation about what learning and teaching can look like.

- Make the conversation come from a place of questioning. If the conversations in which we engage around education are nothing more than us making declarative statements about the way things should be and what others need, we're not setting ourselves up to learn. By asking people who hold different perspectives to share their understandings of needs and their ideas for what will best serve to meet those needs, you're opening up to new understandings.

—— 3 ——

⌖

Citizenship Is More Important Than the Workforce

There's a movement afoot that says school should prepare kids for the twenty-first century workforce. And on its surface, that seems like a good goal. Who could argue with that? Kids are going to need jobs when they graduate, especially in a time when economic stability seems precarious at best.

But focusing on workforce development sells our students short. It assumes that the most we can hope for our students is a life of work when there is so much more to learn. The purpose of public education is not the creation of the twenty-first-century workforce, but rather, the cocreation—in conjunction with our students—of twenty-first century citizens. "Worker" is, without question, a subset of "citizen"; and if we aim for "citizen," we'll get the workforce we need, but aiming only for creating workers won't get our society the citizens it needs.

A public education centered primarily on workforce development will put a high premium on following directions and doing what you're told. A public education centered on citizenship development will still teach rules, but it will teach students to question the ideas underlying those rules. Workforce development will reinforce the hierarchies that we see in most corporate cultures, whereas a citizenship focus will teach students that their voices matter, regardless of station.

It's not only about what society needs, it's also about what students need. We can completely change the lens of "Why do we need to study this?" when the answer deals with being an informed and active citizen as opposed to what we need to know to do our work. Most people don't need to know calculus, the periodic table of elements, the date of the signing of the Magna Carta, or *Hamlet* to be a good worker. But you do need to understand statistical analysis to read fivethirtyeight.com and make sense of the sociopolitical conversations there. You do need to understand basic chemistry to understand how an oil spill from the *Exxon Valdez* affects the region. Understanding how England evolved from a pure aristocracy to a constitutional monarchy, which helped sow the seeds of American democracy, helps us to make sense of our own country's history. And understanding how Hamlet chooses action or inaction in the famous "To be or not to be" soliloquy might help us make better choices in our own lives. The goal of a citizenship-driven education exposes students to ideas that will challenge them, push them, and help them to make sense of a confusing world.

And more to the point—when we do this, we don't lie to kids when we say that's what high school is for.

Our society is changing, and there are some serious warning signs that our economy may be fundamentally shifting in ways that will make it more and more difficult for education to be "the great equalizer." Children across the socioeconomic spectrum are realizing that the economic "sell" of public education isn't ringing true. As college costs creep over $200,000 for private four-year colleges and over $100,000 for public colleges (for example, in 2014 Penn State's costs, with room and board, were $28,000 per year in state[4]) and as more jobs move to labor markets that do not have the high wages of the United States, the idea that all kids who work hard in high school will go to college and have economic success in life is an uglier and uglier lie.

We're going to have some deeply challenging problems to solve in the near future, and we think that we're going to be faced with hard choices about our lives. We want our schools to help students be ready to solve those problems, to weigh in on those problems, and to vote on those problems. That's why history and science are so important. It's why kids have to learn how to create and present their ideas in powerful ways. It's why kids have to become critical consumers and producers of information. And hopefully, along the way, they find the careers that will help them build sustainable, enjoyable, productive lives.

We want to be honest about why we teach what we teach. We're tired of schools and politicians implicitly promising that the result of successful schooling is high wages. And we're tired of too many adults forgetting everything else that goes into helping people realize their potential in the process.

Teaching kids that hard work in school will mean more money is a shortcut and an example of the shoddy logic that doesn't ring true to many kids. Most kids—especially in our cities—know someone who did everything they were supposed to do but still struggled to achieve in their lives after school.

Teaching kids that hard work in school will help them develop skills that will help them be more fully realized citizens and people is—without question—a harder argument to make, but it stands a much better chance of being true.

From Theory to Practice

- Ask the question, "How does my 'class/school/district/home' help kids to become fully realized citizens of the world, and how does it not?" Examine practices that are unhelpful in fulfilling that goal and work to change them.

- Work to create opportunities for students to engage in civic-minded projects both inside and outside the school so that students can see the work they do in the wider world.

—— 4 ——

Build Modern Schools

We talk a lot about what to call this movement in education. It does seem a little ridiculous to call this the "twenty-first century schools movement" when we're already over a decade into the twenty-first century and we don't really know what we're doing yet. But naming is important, and we should be able to talk meaningfully about what this movement is trying to do and what the goal of all of this actually is. For ourselves, we want to be part of a school movement that recognizes the best of what has come before us and marry that to the best of what we are today. And we think we have an idea of how we want to talk about that.

We want to create modern schools.

For us, the notion of the modern school cuts straight to the heart of what we are trying to do. Modernity is something that we are always striving for, always reinventing, always coming to terms with. We understand the dangers of modernity slipping into post-modernity. This is and should be a valid concern. It should also be a fire under those who are charged with asking, "Are we creating the schools we need today, or have they slipped into yesterday?"

Smart modernists understand that they stand on the shoulders of giants. Modern schools should not denigrate the past, nor should they ignore what has come before them. The modernist learns from history and builds upon it. Those are the goals we want to have. And we believe that is a powerful lens for our children. Moreover, the idea of modern schools encompasses not just the tools they use, but also the life they lead and the challenges they face. It recognizes that school is about now and their future while honoring and learning from the past.

A modern school movement does not assume that because we learned a certain way when we were kids, our children must learn the same. A modern school movement does not assume that what was good for us will automatically be good for our kids, nor does it assume that just because we did something a certain way in the past that it holds no value in the future. The modern school movement does not have to focus solely on tools or skills; rather, it can also focus on ideas and people and the lives we live today.

We want to create modern schools, in and of our time, for our time, for these kids.

From Theory to Practice

- Examine one way your life has changed over the past ten years due to a change in society. Is there a parallel to that change in your school? Could there be?

- What is a process in your teaching that is grounded in older practice that, while still worthwhile, could be reinvigorated by examining its relevance to the world we live in today?

————— 5 —————

Be One School

You have to be one school.

A brilliant example of how not to do this can be found in the August 29, 2011 *Salon.com* article, "Confessions of a Bad Teacher."[5] In it, a would-be career changer details his one semester as a teacher in a New York City school. He talks about his struggles with classroom management and how his principal was of little support:

> A large, round woman in her late 30s, Ms. P kept her hair pulled back tightly. Her eyebrows were long, thin and very expressive, moving up and down like a caffeinated drawbridge. Ms. P's large mouth, set between grapefruit-size cheeks, was in a constant frown. At least, that's all I ever saw.
>
> "What was that you were trying to do?" she asked the next day in her office, not waiting for my answer. "Assign the children seats?"
>
> My effort at classroom management was dismissed for what it was—a total failure. I told her about detention, dean's referrals and my conversation with Mr. Rashid. She waved her hand.
>
> "You need to have lunch with the girls," she said. "You need to show them that you care about them."
>
> I realized I was living a nightmare.

If taking a student who isn't being productive in class out to lunch to get to know the student better is a good thing (and we believe it is), then shouldn't principals and teachers share lunches and learn about each other's needs and ideas?

The writer had a bad boss, yes, but not in the way he thinks he did. It's not that he got bad advice; it's that there was a profound disconnect between what the administrator wanted for the children of her school and what the administrator wanted for her teachers.

It's hard sometimes. Teachers are adults, and they get paid. So, as administrators, we want and expect more from them. But the values that administrators hold will be reflected in the values teachers manifest when they work with the kids. Both kindness and cruelty flow downstream.

You cannot want one thing for students and another for teachers. The principal in the article tried to bully the teacher into caring about the kids, when everything we see about her behavior showed that she did not care about the development of this teacher.

If we want classrooms to be active places, our faculty meetings must also be active.

If we want students to feel cared for by teachers, then we must care for teachers.

If we want students to be able to engage in powerful inquiry, so must teachers.

The biggest crime of the story is that the principal wanted the teachers to treat the students with kindness and caring, but was unwilling to do the same for the adults in her care.

We must endeavor to be one school.

From Theory to Practice

- What do you do in your work that you would not allow your students to do? Could you allow your students to have a process that is more aligned with the process you most want for yourself?

- Examine the guidelines—explicit or implicit—that govern the expected behaviors of various stakeholders in your classroom or your school. Are they the same? Could they be?

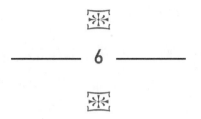

Vision Must Live in Practice

Many schools have mission and vision statements. Some of those schools also have a listing of core values. Within this subset, we might even find a collection of schools who have drafted essential questions.

What is painfully, distressingly, and alarmingly true about many of these schools is the proportion of them that draft these well-meaning documents, file them, and never ever return to them again—until it's time to craft some sort of improvement plan. This is only slightly better than those who print these driving statements on banners for all who visit to notice, while their actions are in stark contrast with the values literally hanging over their heads.

Vision must live in practice.

The same is true of missions, values, and driving questions.

At Science Leadership Academy (SLA), a Philadelphia high school opened in September 2006, these three driving questions form the basis of instruction:

"How do we *learn*?"
"What can we *create*?"
"What does it mean to *lead*?"

SLA is built on the notion that inquiry is the very first step in the process of learning. Developed in partnership with The Franklin Institute and its commitment to inquiry-based science, SLA provides a rigorous college-preparatory curriculum with a focus on science, technology, mathematics, and entrepreneurship. Students at SLA learn in a project-based environment where the core values of *inquiry, research, collaboration, presentation*, and *reflection* are emphasized in all classes.

The structure of SLA reflects its core values, with longer class periods to allow for more laboratory work in science classes and performance-based learning in all classes. In addition, students in the upper grades have more flexible schedules to allow for opportunities for dual enrollment programs with area universities and career development internships in laboratory and business settings, as well as with The Franklin Institute.

At SLA, learning is not just something that happens from 8:30 A.M. to 3:00 P.M., but a continuous process that expands beyond the four walls of the classroom into every facet of our lives.[6]

At SLA, we work to constantly ask how the school's core values of inquiry, research, collaboration, presentation, and reflection can be seen in the learning experiences designed for our students. While not every piece of work that students complete speaks to each of the core values, by continually asking the question of how what we are doing fits with our core values we help to ensure we are constantly practicing those things we purport to value most.

The vision of a school can live in practice only if it is shared by all within the community. We have seen many schools where teachers arrive for their first professional development day of the new school year, sip coffee from industrial-sized mugs, and listen as the school's principal stands before them and explains the vision for the new school year. Often, too often, this is a vision devoid of any remnants of the vision of the previous school year, or the year before that.

While it is understandable for a principal to endeavor to energize his or her faculty at the start of the new year, shifting course dramatically and often will only lead teachers to pay lip service to the "new" vision while resorting to those goals and values they find most comfortable when they return to their classrooms.

Schools would be better off finding a vision in which the desired practice of a school can truly take root and then seeking ways to embody that vision in every action of every individual on the campus. Once that has happened, the next step is not to find a new way of saying what you believe, but rather to deepen the expressions of those beliefs and values key to your institution's identity.

We are better off figuring out how to say the things we believe and actually do than finding new things to say.

Coming to terms with what a school believes as a learning organization is a strong first step toward making the change. As with so many journeys, it is the steps that follow that determine what you will become.

When vision is put into practice, when who we want to be is constantly reflected in our practice, then we can move closer to the better versions of ourselves and our institutions.

From Theory to Practice

- Dust off your school's mission, vision, values, and so on.
  Over the course of a semester, dedicate meeting time
  to defining what actions and habits of mind would be
  visible at the school if all of the adults in the community
  committed to enacting these espoused beliefs.

- Once you've outlined what it will look like, put those visions into practice and carve out time to share what you've observed throughout the school. Give colleagues an opportunity to share the successes and positive actions of their peers. Commit to keeping at least a few minutes of time sacred in every group meeting and share, in these moments, how the core beliefs are manifested in action. Doing this will help to prevent your school from regressing to the average.

- We realize not everyone reading these words will be in a position of leadership at their school or have control over meeting agendas on a school-wide scale. That's fine. Start the change small, show its effectiveness, and build from there. Although you may not control formal meetings, find a group of colleagues within your school with whom you share common purpose and begin thinking about becoming a school of one from small beginnings.

———— 7 ————

We Must Blend Theory and Practice

There is a movement in some parts of the country to pre-pare future classroom teachers without regard to those educational thinkers who have come before. Programs such as the Relay Graduate School of Education[7] in New York have ignored the importance of a balance of theory and practice in teaching and learning, and opted instead for a focus on practice alone. In order to build the schools we need, a regard for theory put into practice and then researched as reflection is paramount. Only through the blending of theory and practice can we move toward teachers who are both thoughtfully reflective about their practice as well as adept at developing new practices based on their students' needs. Graduate education programs that focus primarily on practice and turn a blind eye to the study of pedagogical theory cite the needs of beginning teachers to enter their classrooms with tools to help their students learn.

What happens, though, when the novice teacher has tried each of the forty-nine techniques offered in Doug Lemov's *Teach Like a Champion*[8] and finds himself in need of a fiftieth? It is possible this teacher will begin to look more deeply at the forty-nine practices in his repertoire and then begin to suss out the underlying theories of learning that guide those practices. But then again, he might not. This should not be left to chance.

The study of great and deep thinkers like John Dewey, Jean Piaget, Seymour Papert, Magdelene Lampert, Theodore Sizer, Sara Lawrence-Lightfoot, and Carol Dweck, alongside the learning of a collection of beginning practices, enables novice teachers to enter the classroom feeling prepared, and also allows them to think critically about their own practice when they find the tools with which they left their graduate programs to be lacking. Teachers who might otherwise feel they are discovering the practice of teaching and learning in a vacuum would do well to carry with them reminders that wise minds have spent their careers thinking and writing about the very dilemmas facing teachers in modern classrooms.

Historical understanding does more than let teachers know they are not going it alone when they enter their classrooms. Understanding the theories of learning, investigating the theorists who developed them, and then working to synthesize that knowledge into a coherent personal philosophy and teaching practice demands that teachers be more thoughtful about their practice, make choices through critical analysis of evidence, and back their practice in reasoned arguments—in short, to engage in the type of thinking we hope they will seek to elicit from their students.

By asking how children learn, how others have suggested children learn, and how teaching might assist in that learning, teachers are compelled to train their minds to think critically and to put a premium on asking questions and seeking answers. This is different from a practice built on the largely unthinking deployment of a set of prepackaged "tools" delivered absent any question of why they are being used.

Teaching is complex; we are not arguing that teachers well versed in the study of the history of learning theory and various pedagogies can simply enter a classroom, develop a curriculum, and implement that curriculum in such a way that all students in the class are enthralled, enlightened, and driven to answer questions. Quite the opposite. Rather, we argue that teachers should learn the pedagogy of those who have come before concurrently with learning those practices thought to be most effective for beginning teachers.

What's more, it is likely that the critical thinking required to blend pedagogy and practice in whatever context a teacher finds herself will lead to an inquiry-driven practice. Although inquiry on the part of teachers does not ensure that those teachers will include inquiry and critical thought in their classrooms, it does make such an overflow more likely than if teachers are using the plug 'n' chug method of practice without theory.

From Theory to Practice

- Draft a theory of learning. This can be done as a department, as a school, or as an individual. For most teachers, answering the question, "How do students learn best?" is something they've not done since they were completing their preservice training, if at all. Sitting down and writing what we believe about learning can be an eye-opening act, and when shared with peers it will create deep discussion.

- Ask why you're doing what you're doing. Classroom life can be hectic. Moving through a day charged with the care of a group of young people often means we pick up tricks and practices in the moment that we unthinkingly allow to become habits. Consider a practice you frequently deploy in teaching and ask, "Why do I do this? How does it sync with what I believe about learning?" Whatever the answers, they are guaranteed to lead to a more thoughtful set of teaching practices. If you have difficulty picking a practice, ask a colleague to observe a class in your room, documenting everything you do and say. This running log will likely lead you to see what you're doing from a new angle. Another option is to video yourself teaching a class and find your practice that way. Whatever you choose, find a practice, and ask why. Rich conversation and reflection will follow.

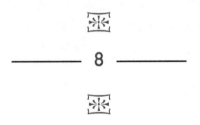

———— 8 ————

Everything Matters

Go into almost any school today, and you will find a hodgepodge of programs—behavioral, administrative, extracurricular, and curricular. At some schools each program has a language all its own, and there's rarely a guarantee that the parts added together make a greater whole. At other schools, you have processes and procedures that exist for not much more reason than "That is the way they have existed for as long as anyone can remember." What we need are schools that are much more of a unified whole, where a vision—and a plan to enact that vision—drives what everyone does.

Many people seem to think that curriculum and pedagogy can be divorced from the other school systems and structures—food service and discipline and parent relationships and hiring and the dozens of other processes and interactions that happen in schools. In our experience, that is not the case. When you have a vision for what a school can be, it has to permeate every pore of the school. Every process, every interaction, every system needs to be held to that process. And although there are pieces of the school that may be only tangential to the mission, it is important to go through the process of examining how the core vision of the school affects each part of the school.

This is especially true when you move to a more inquiry-driven, student-empowered school. It really does affect everything. When students become empowered to ask questions and seek out answers, everything changes, and you cannot—and should not—think that you can leave inquiry at the classroom door. When teachers see themselves as learners and researchers and planners, they will question traditions and policies. And as a community, everyone has to learn how to bring these ideas to bear to make the school whole.

We must understand that this is what is needed to make schools into better, healthier, more authentic places. We can all agree that getting more amazing people into our schools would be great (and yes, there are some people working as teachers who should not be), but to think that this overly simplistic "more good, less bad" argument is enough for our schools is dangerously misguided for any number of reasons. One of the main points of this book is this: teaching is not an individual affair—or at least it shouldn't be. Teachers are better when they work collaboratively, but even more than that, teachers teach better and students learn more when the school has a vision that actually means something and a plan to make that vision a reality.

Right now, the overriding mythos around teaching is the hero myth—the story of that one amazing teacher who can change a child's life, make a difference, and then get played in a movie by Hilary Swank or Edward James Olmos. And though yes, there are teachers filling that role in schools across the country every day, that is not the path to a systemic reform. There are over 3,700,000 teachers in America,[9] and under the best of circumstances—and we are not in the best of circumstances these days—it is unrealistic to think all 3,700,000 teachers will be those "amazing" teachers who have a seemingly never-ending store of energy and passion for the kids. And, for the record, it is worth asking how that model is sustainable for all but a very few.

We need to figure out how to build systems and structures that allow good people of honest intent to do great things together. It is realistic to assume that we can build an educational system in this country around good people and smart systems. That does not mean the system needs to be teacher-proof. And it does not mean creating standardized content that strips the job of all of its creativity and passion and joy. Rather, it means understanding that people work best in service of something that they can believe in, when there is a pathway toward excellence and they can collaborate. Good people are capable of great things under the right circumstances. But absent those circumstances, schools will squander the good will and best intentions of everyone—students and teachers—who works there.

From Theory to Practice

- Give space to new ideas. For school administrators, this means clearing agenda time across any number of regularly scheduled meetings and asking people to share. In some schools, sharing becomes a laundry list of complaints. Prevent that by asking specific questions:

- What are you excited about that's happening with your students right now?
- What questions are you working to answer in your practice?
- What would you like to build and teach together?

- Rethink schedules to be in service of learning and teaching. At SLA much pain went into efforts to create common planning time for teachers within a subject area. In planning periods, teachers invite one another in to see and share practices, and time is carved out weekly for the faculty to meet and think about who we are as a school and what we are doing to fulfill our mission. Keeping in mind who you want to be as a place of learning and what you want for teachers and students, start to think about how your school day could better serve that mission.

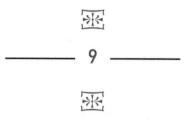

"What's Good?" Is Better Than "What's New?"

We live in amazing times—times of faster technological change than ever seen before in human history. And with that technological change have come incredible changes in the way we live our lives.

Although schools are historically slow to change, we are now seeing rapid changes in the way schools operate. More students are taking courses online. Teachers are bringing new technologies into the classroom every day. And the digitization of student performance has led to a new focus on analysis of data in ways never seen before.

While we should be sure our schools evolve to accommodate these changes and work to incorporate new ideas into our schools, we should also remember that very smart people were teaching before us. In our haste to rush to the new, the shiny, we must not forget the lessons learned in the past.

To that end, we must be scholars of our own profession. We must work to understand the reasons that schools have become the institutions they are and how innovation has—and has not—happened before. When we do, we will be more equipped to innovate and evolve.

We cannot blindly follow whatever trend is hot this week, changing when the trend fades and leaving schools always playing catch-up.

The best policies and practices are created by taking the best ideas of the past and marrying them to the world we live in today. We can create something new, grounded in the best of what we have been, but with an eye toward what our kids need to become today. To that end, when we look to innovate, we must ask ourselves "What's good?" more than we ask ourselves "What's new?"

New fades. Good endures. That is a goal worth chasing.

From Theory to Practice

- Read some other books about school. Our history is often unknown to us, not because it has not been collected but because we have not endeavored to learn it. We recommend three books to familiarize yourself with the why and how of school history: Dan Lortie's *Schoolteacher* (2002), Larry Cuban and David Tyack's *Tinkering toward Utopia* (1995), and Dana Goldstein's *Teacher Wars* (2014).

- When you think you have a grasp of those who have come before and how we got to where we are now, join a professional organization and imbue it with the history and purpose you bring. Every content area has its own professional organization, and there are myriad others dedicated to professional learning, reform, and so on. Before joining, be sure to read the mission and vision of any organization to make sure they and you are thinking in the same direction.

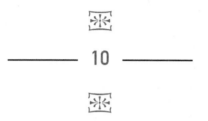

Reflection Means Better, Not More

One of the most important questions any school or teacher can ask is simple: "How can we be more thoughtful about what we do?" Unfortunately, it's not the question we ask most frequently. The question schools and teachers have fallen in love with—"What more should we be doing?"—is much more dangerous and leads to the creation of unsustainable systems.

Without a doubt, there's a space for the question of what more schools can be doing to improve how they serve children and adults, but this thinking leads quickly to a list of things that can't be done because of limited resources or capacity. It leads to a kind of deficit thinking that works against any hopes of institutional optimism. Schools are defeated before they've even identified what it is they're attempting to accomplish.

The better question, the sustainable question, the question that frees up resources for schools to do more is the question of reflection and refinement.

By asking how they can be more thoughtful about their practices, schools turn their thinking inward and resist a cycle of adoption of and overload around whatever new and shiny program or product promises to improve student achievement.

Imagine the principal who announces to the faculty at the beginning of the year, "This year, we won't be adopting any new programs. Instead, we'll be spending the next months getting better at what we already do." Imagine the relief of the teachers. They would have the space and mandate not to do more, but to do better.

We know a supervisor of preservice teachers who remarked on how difficult it was proving for him to get his student teachers to reflect deeply on what was happening in their classrooms. They were focused on the next day and the day after that and the day after that. Stopping to think about what had just happened, what had worked and what hadn't, held little appeal. They had things to do, and those things didn't include worrying about the things they had already done. It didn't occur to them that thinking about how they could have done better might translate to doing better the next time.

For the supervising teacher, though, reflection was the most important tool he could help these student teachers refine and implement. If he could help those in his charge start down the road of reflective practice, he would know he had made a lasting impact.

Such is the case in the life of any teacher. Schools are better when they create spaces and expectations for reflection.

Formalized protocols for the adoption of reflective practices abound—the National School Reform Faculty protocols[10] are a wonderful resource—but amazing progress can be made without them. What is necessary, as with most deepening ideas, is the space and support for reflecting on the work being done. Imagine our hypothetical principal committing twenty minutes of each faculty meeting to teachers' writing and reflecting on a single lesson from their week. Imagine if this same principal realized the importance of modeling this expectation for the school's teachers and published a blog of her reflections publicly for all her teachers to see.

While it would be ideal if this reflective practice started with the principal, it could start anywhere. In fact, it should start everywhere. Department chairs, classroom teachers, sports coaches—they can all be models of reflection to those with whom they work. They can all drive the improvement of practice.

As the supervising teacher understood, reflection means softening and sanding down the edges of instructional practices to make them fit together more easily. Reflective practice means asking not "What more can we be doing?" but "How can we do what we're already doing, better?"

From Theory to Practice

- Start with what you're doing well. In a recent meeting of English teachers in a district who would be moving from print to digital textbooks, we asked first, "What are you already doing that you want to make sure you keep doing as you begin to adopt these new tools?" Keeping track of what's working in the midst of change can help keep your room or your building grounded in a sense of self that's helpful.

- Keep what you're improving in perspective, and the scope in check. If you decide to improve a bevy of practices and programs, it's the same as deciding to add a few programs to the way of doing school. Remember capacity.

- Examine the National School Reform Faculty protocols. Not all of them will feel right, but you may find some that will help you and your colleagues jump-start the reflective process. Reflection is not something that comes easily to many people, so having a set of protocols that help teachers get away from the blank page can be just the thing to inspire powerful critical analysis of practice.

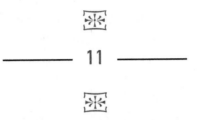

11

Consider the Worst Consequence of Your Best Idea

You have to wonder why desks in rows, textbooks, and teachers standing by a black-, white-, or smart board have survived as long as they have as the dominant instructional models when so few people think that it's actually a good way to teach and learn.

Then you realize that while it never goes all that right, it rarely goes all that wrong either. Teachers don't usually get in trouble when administrators walk into their classroom and see kids with books open, doing work, even if the work isn't worth doing.

And all those other ideas that we love so much—inquiry, project-based learning, technology, real-world application of student work—they get so ... messy. Something always seems to go wrong. And we have to face the fact that education is a somewhat reactionary field to work in. So many good ideas die when something goes wrong and someone decides that we should never do *that* again.

So the desks get put back into rows, and the textbooks land on the desks again, and the teacher goes back to lecturing the class.

But there's a way around that, and it involves thoughtful planning. It doesn't involve coming up with the perfect idea, because let's be clear—there is no perfect idea. Everything has a downside.

At SLA, for example, the best thing about our school is the incredible empowerment of our students. And the downside of that is that those same kids who are so incredibly empowered occasionally start to feel really entitled, and then we have to deal with that.

But we realized that would happen before we started. And every time it does happen, we remind ourselves that it is a natural consequence of what we love. Our reaction has to be tempered so we don't lose the soul of our school.

So whenever you have a new idea, ask yourself:

"What is the worst consequence of my best idea? What is the thing that, even if we do this really well, will frustrate me, frustrate kids, frustrate parents? How can this go wrong by going right?"

Then follow up with these questions: "How will we, as a community, mitigate that consequence? What are we willing to live with, if it means we get something incredible out of it as well? What risks are we willing to take? How will we front-load the negative possibilities of this idea to our stakeholders so they are prepared for it as well?"

Don't do this alone. Do this as a community, because the author of an idea is often the last person to see the scary side of the idea. Do this not so you can just dismiss fear, but so you can acknowledge it and lessen the factors that cause it.

Most of the time, there is still the thing you didn't think of. But the very act of going through the iterative process of trying to solve problems before they show up has made us more willing to acknowledge that our ideas aren't perfect and that problem solving will always be necessary. The goal isn't perfection—it's pragmatism.

Whether it is a new technology, a new pedagogy, or a new program in the school, we have to be thoughtful in the way we evolve as schools. We have to acknowledge the good and bad in the changes we make if we are to do right by the kids in our charge. And we have to own the limits of our ideas, so that we can hold onto those ideas and not regress to a vision of school that, while easily recognized, is loved by no one. Owning our flaws and learning what we can mitigate and what we have to live with is a way to power past fear once and for all.

An easy, concrete example for us was thinking through the policies around being a one-to-one laptop school. We made a decision not to lock down the machines, because we wanted the kids to really feel like they could use the laptops to their fullest potential. That meant that the kids went home with a fully unlocked laptop to unfiltered home networks. We had to talk to students and parents beforehand about issues of internet porn, good digital citizenship, and being safe and smart with your digital footprint.

Then we had to expect that no matter how much we did that, kids would make mistakes. And because we agreed, as a community, that the benefits of all the kids being able to access the full power of the laptop outweighed the negatives of some of the kids using the laptops inappropriately, the laptops are still open seven years later. And we're better for it.

From Theory to Practice

- Make collaborative troubleshooting part of every design process. Getting outside eyes on an idea will almost always bring up challenges that the author did not anticipate.

- Remember to consider what will be problematic even if the idea goes exactly right. Owning that our ideas are not perfect and that there are no panaceas in education (or life) is an important way to build smart systems that keep everyone healthy and humble.

- Involve the kids. Ask them for their answers to the question of "What is the worst consequence of your best idea?" They will bring a much-needed perspective to the idea.

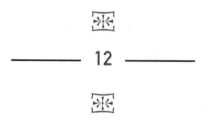

Disrupt Disruption

With the publication of *Disrupting Class* in 2008, Clayton Christensen and Michael Horn introduced the idea of disruption to the education world, and the effects have been, well, disruptive.

The people driving school policy, from the Boston Consulting Group to the Gates Foundation to the venture capitalists at GSV Advisors, are now rushing to disrupt schools, pushing a faster rate of change and an increasing corporatization of the education sector. In states and districts all over America the disruption has occurred, as funding for anything not championed by big business or the federal government has dried up, leading to layoffs, school closures, and profound instability in what has been, for nearly one hundred years, one of the more stable institutions in American culture—the school.

But why were we—the tech-savvy educators—so quick to fall in love with the idea of disruption as Christensen presented it? Behind the idea that technology was going to change our schools—it can, it should, it is changing them—was a market-driven vision of school that opened the door to disruption as a positive force in education.

When was the last time any teacher thought that disruption was a positive force in a child's life?

The time has come for us to retake the language of school reform. Words like "disruption" and "revolution" create a mindset among reformers that make it OK to cut budgets, lay off teachers, close schools, and—at root—implement high-speed, high-stakes changes without fully examining the worst consequences of their own ideas. After all, there's usually a body count in revolutions, and disruption always makes people uncomfortable for a little while, right? But we have to stop thinking that's OK.

Moreover, revolutionaries and disrupters have little use for history and context. After all, what they are creating will be totally new, right? Why would disrupters have to immerse themselves in the history of education when what they are creating is so tech-savvy and new that it will be unlike anything we've seen before?

To wit—those who think that they can come in from the outside of educational systems and disrupt schools are engaging in a profound act of hubris. Sadly, it's rare that the reformers are the ones who suffer when the reforms prove less than successful.

It's the kids who do. The reformers go back to the world of business or on to their next cause. And they get to throw up their hands and say, "If we couldn't fix our broken schools, it's not our fault. It just means no one can save them." And that, of course, only serves to reinforce the notion that we should just blow the whole thing up and start over anyway.

We can aspire to more than that.

What we want in our schools is not disruption, but evolution. Our schools cannot stay static—on this we can agree—but disruption and revolution are the wrong models. We want our schools to *evolve*. We need to grow; we need to take the best of what we have been and marry those ideas to the new world in which we live. The patterns of the growth of our educational systems should follow a logical path, with as few disruptions as we can manage.

We owe it to all of the people—students, teachers, parents— who bring the best of themselves to the flawed systems of school every day to make those systems better tomorrow than they are today. But we also owe it to those people to make that evolution as painless as possible, so that the upheaval and disruption do not mean the loss of dignity and learning and care for the people who inhabit our schools.

From Theory to Practice

- This is a combination of working toward evolution of your systems and considering the unintended consequences of what we are doing. As you work to make changes in your classroom, your school, and your district, consider the reasons for those changes, and ask yourself, "Will what I am proposing move the systems it affects forward in a positive way?"

- Consider how those you disrupt may or may not be able to contribute to the process, and adjust accordingly. In the communities we strive to create, those present will have the voice necessary to contribute to decision making. Not all systems start that way. To make sure the changes you are proposing (disruptive or not) are informed by all involved, it will be helpful to engage in a power-mapping session to create a visual model of everyone who holds a stake in your learning space and to outline each person's or group's power to speak up and make decisions within the system. There are many tools for this process, and simply participating in the process is enough. If you need to find a place to start, the folks at MoveOn.org[11] have outlined the power-mapping process in easy-to-follow steps. Feel free to adjust for a school setting as necessary.

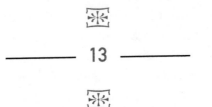

—————— 13 ——————

Humility Matters

The death of any great idea occurs the moment its inventor falls in love with it.

The death of any great student occurs when she decides she is smarter than all her classmates and therefore has nothing to learn from them.

The death of any great teacher takes place when he falls in love with the sound of his own voice and stops hearing the voices of the students who would do more than parrot the teacher's voice back at him.

The death of any great principal happens when she thinks she is the only one who can move the school forward and stops listening to the students, teachers, and parents she serves.

The work of teaching and learning is hard. It requires courage on the part of everyone involved to take the kind of risks necessary for real learning to happen. That kind of courage can also create surety that is dangerous. We have to understand it, because it is rampant in schools of all kinds, but we also have to work to combat it when we see it in others and in ourselves.

Real strength—the kind that doesn't come because one has a title of "principal" or "teacher" or "honor roll student" or even (or perhaps especially) "education reformer"—requires an almost Zen-like state in which we operate from a centered core that makes us confident enough to listen to dissent and difference.

But humility isn't only about listening to dissent. It's about giving up control. It's about stepping back and letting others do for themselves. It's about letting people own their ideas and create things of which you yourself never would have conceived. It means knowing enough not to presume that you know every outcome. And it even means, sometimes, giving up things we love doing so that others can do them too.

Sometimes we have to learn those moments the hard way. When Chris was a young English teacher, he tried to give extensive feedback on every draft of every paper his students wrote. They needed him to do that for them. He was the teacher, and he understood better than anyone else in that classroom what good writing looked like.

Except that as he tried to keep up with the paper load, he wasn't sleeping.

So he tried peer editing, remembering it from a graduate school class. And then he noticed something—the comments kids made were different than his, perhaps, but they weren't worse. In fact, in many cases, the students had insight into each other's work that he didn't have. And the kids realized that they could help each other, and that might have been more important than any comma splice that Chris would have caught. Suddenly, Chris had to admit that he wasn't the only expert voice in the room. He couldn't be that "hero teacher" who would single-handedly teach all the kids to write.

What a wonderful myth to have to give up.

And that taught Chris another profound lesson about humility. True humility means understanding that one's personal empowerment doesn't ever have to come at the expense of someone else's empowerment. There's enough to go around.

From Theory to Practice

- Ask what you can give up. In every educator's practice, there are ways of doing things adopted long ago with no clear reason why they are perpetuated in current practice. Find a thing you do and ask how you can take yourself out of the process. It may be that you fancy yourself a fantastic former of groups for student work. Stop that. Maybe you outline every deadline for a large project to the minute. Stop that. Give students a general overview of what needs to be done and the final date for submission of an assignment. Then give some time and space to allow them to set their own mini deadlines. This removes the presumption that all we ask students to do is all that life asks students to do, and instead gives them the power to find and make the time they need.

- Invite someone in. This could be inviting a fellow teacher to come view your teaching with an eye toward talking about it afterward, or it could be a principal asking teachers to take a look at a meeting agenda with an eye toward what's right, what's wrong, and what's missing. Wherever you have a mind-set of "I've got this," that's probably the right place to take a humble look at how others can help you improve the practice.

- Ask the kids in a "no-gotcha" environment. Create an anonymous survey, using tools like Google Forms or SurveyMonkey, that allows the class to give you honest feedback without fear of reprisal. Ask good questions such as, "What works for you in my classroom?" "What doesn't work in my classroom?" "What do you do if you struggle?" "What are the three words you think of when you think of this class?"

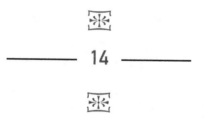

Build Consensus

One of the most challenging questions about the path we've walked at SLA is "Yes, but what about those of us who don't get to start from scratch?"

It's a fair question, and while we believe it is possible—in fact, necessary—for existing schools to change to become more humane, forward-thinking institutions, there's no question that those schools have a disadvantage that we don't have. Although we do always point out that starting a school from scratch, while having many advantages, also means that you must reinvent every traditional process, from curriculum design to the ways in which faculty place orders for classroom supplies when we run out.

But the more we talk to people about the ways we established norms at SLA—the ways we got everyone to pull in the same direction on curriculum and assessment—the more we have come to believe that our greatest strength is also the necessary first step for schools and leaders who *aren't* starting from the beginning. It is our willingness to commit to consensus-driven decision making.

The hardest part about building a school around a vision is agreeing on how that vision looks in reality. Sometimes agreeing on the vision is actually the easy part. It is moving from a vision statement or a set of shared principles to a reality that is really difficult. That's still a challenge we face at SLA, but it is something that really cannot be given short shrift if our school—any school—is to remain healthy and true to a vision.

The key is consensus-driven decision making. If we wish to reform existing schools, we must be willing to take a broad vision and then let that vision be embraced by all stakeholders … and not just the big ideas, but any of the important implementation pieces as well.

So what does consensus-driven decision making look like? First, it's important to understand that it does not mean that everyone agrees with every decision. That's just about impossible. What it means is that everyone agrees to live with and abide by decisions, and everyone trusts the process enough to know that all of us have both moments when we give up our sacred cow and moments when our idea forms the backbone of what we decide.

Perhaps most important, consensus-driven decision making means that when there are disagreements and concerns, those concerns are aired, and attempts must be made to both address and ameliorate them. People have to commit to the idea that we'll all sit around the table until everyone feels comfortable moving forward. And people have to commit to being willing to listen and move forward. The statement "I agree to move forward" is incredibly powerful.

This isn't the kind of thing that people learn and trust overnight. It's not something that you can just decide, "OK, now we're going to do this. Everyone, get on board." It takes a ton of time. It is the kind of thing that can make some people decide to leave when an organization is obviously pulling away from their core beliefs. But it can also make schools healthy, strong places. The up-front work of building consensus can lead to all kinds of amazing leaps forward when it comes time for implementation. It can build trust, and it can build community.

People have to realize that in this kind of process they must be willing to build a *true* synthesis of ideas. This can go horribly awry when the process produces some sort of fifteen-headed monster because, to appease everyone, everyone's idea got stuck onto the main idea. You end up with a completely unworkable idea that bears no resemblance to the original. For consensus to work, people must be willing to change and compromise; to listen to opposing ideas, find common ground, and work from there. It doesn't work any other way.

In time, we have found that folks begin to trust the process enough that the meetings do get shorter. For example, our discussions about our senior Capstone Project[12]—a year-long inquiry project that all SLA seniors undertake—have been amazing in that one person comes to the table with a general framework, many ideas are tossed around, and then folks do reach a point where they trust the process enough to say either "Hey, I'm going to put some time in on the committee to revise what we've got and represent it," or "I was heard; now let's see where we go."

When we first started discussing Capstone, there was a movement to make all Capstone projects STEM-related. However, through the process we came to understand that constraint was limiting our students' ideas and creativity, and it fell by the wayside.

But by taking the time to play with the idea, discuss it, and agree to move past it, everyone involved—including the originators of the idea—left the process feeling that what had come out of it was where we had needed to go.

That's not to say that everyone agreed with how our Capstone process came to fruition. Some people argued for more structure. Other people were concerned that our advisory system could not support the process. But incorporating those ideas into the Capstone process requires time and effort, and people must decide whether they feel strongly enough about their issues to join up and make the process better. Those who felt strongly enough joined the committee, and their work was reflected in the way Capstone is now done at SLA.

Building consensus is hard work, and we all have plenty of moments when we think that it would be easier if everyone just did it the way we wanted it done. But at SLA we've always been pleased with the outcome of this process; not always right away, but eventually. It means that everyone—principal included—has to have a strong enough ego to be keep their ego out of the process. And everyone has to really be willing to listen. This means that, in the end, you can get to a point where everyone does indeed agree on how to move forward. And that's how change can start.

From Theory to Practice

- Give the process space and time. Many times, consensus isn't part of a school's way of doing things, because decisions are made at break-neck pace. For some matters, this is necessary. District paperwork, crisis situations, and the like all demand urgent attention. But when *everything* becomes urgent or all decisions are treated as though they are urgent, the people, and the thoughtfulness they bring, are left out. In working toward consensus, realize the importance of doing things not quickly, but well. A decision or the drafting of a plan may take up space in several meeting agendas before everyone is on board. Give it that space. Better thinking will surely follow.

- Commit. Schools where decisions have been made by decree will need several opportunities to build consensus on several issues for it to become the way of doing business and for trust in the process to accrue. State this from the outset and make the commitment explicit. You'll like the results.

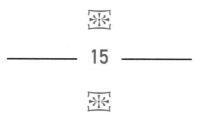

Teach Kids Before Subjects

Ask any teacher what they teach, and you'll get the typical responses:

"I teach science."

"I teach third grade."

"I teach English."

Words matter. And when we give those answers, we miss a chance to humanize our classroom every time.

We should always remember that we teach kids. And that matters. Say the first set of answers out loud and then say the following set out loud.

"I teach kids science."

"I teach third graders."

"I teach kids English."

If we are going to create more student-centered schools, then we need to start by actually mentioning the students when we talk about our classes and our profession. Before we expect everyone to be able to do it, perhaps we should actually say it first.

The point is *not* that the things we teach the kids are unimportant. Science is important. English is important. Third grade is important. But they aren't necessarily important in their abstraction. They have to be important to the kids we teach. It is in the intersection of the kids we teach and the subjects we teach that meaning and learning happen.

What could happen if teachers started using this language? Could it get us to do a better job of seeing the kids in front of us as people, not just as students of a subject? Could it remind us that it isn't enough to love our content, but that we have to love the kids we teach too? Could this be the first step we all agree to take in building human—more humane—schools?

In the end, our kids should never be the implied object of their own education, and we can start changing that with the very language we use to describe what we do.

From Theory to Practice

- When you've completed the drafting of a unit plan or lesson plan, pick a student, then read the plan through the eyes of that student. It doesn't matter if it's a star pupil or the one hanging on the edge of passing; chances are this exercise will help you to see the lesson not through the lens of curriculum, but through the eyes of those you hope will learn the content of that curriculum.

- Commit to telling people you teach children and *then* whatever content area happens to be your specialty, and note the looks on their faces as you answer with words different from their expectations. Pay attention to the curiously difficult and less succinct wording of "I teach sixth graders science." There's something in the awkwardness of saying it that also points to the difficulty and awkwardness inherent in the task, and that's also worth remembering.

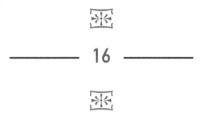

What We Should Ask of Teachers

Conversations abound about what makes a "great" teacher, but very little talk about what that means or how teachers can get there. With that in mind, here's the Top 10 list of what's asked of SLA teachers:

10 Take care of yourself. Teaching is a marathon, not a sprint, and SLA teachers do put themselves out there early and often. We want our teachers to take time for themselves every day. We want SLA teachers to take trips, go to conferences, spend time with family and with each other (*not* talking about school).

9 Understand that your class is but one of five or six or seven classes that kids have and that school is just one

of many things in a teenager's life. While what goes on in your class is important, remember that, at any given moment, there are pressures on your kids' lives that make what goes on in class seem powerfully inconsequential.

8 Never be afraid to bring an idea or a critique or a thought to Chris. Never be afraid to tell him what you think.

7 Be as transparent as possible. That means giving students opportunities to publish their work to the world. That means opening your door to colleagues, to parents, to visitors. That means never playing "gotcha" with the kids with your expectations.

6 Remember that a benevolent dictatorship may make for an orderly class, but it rarely helps kids become better people. Giving kids opportunities to feel ownership of the classroom is important because, in the end, you can get what you want or you can get much more.

5 Remember that inquiry isn't just for kids. If we want our kids to always push themselves to question more, dig deeper, figure it out for themselves, we must be willing to do that too.

4 Take ownership of major pieces of the school outside your classroom. SLA works because everyone takes on pieces of it. Run a club, chair a committee, write a grant, do the thing you always wanted to do in a school but never thought the structure of school could support.

3 Be part of a community of teachers and learners and speak the same language. Kids spend too much time in schools figuring out their teachers, and that detracts from the powerful work they can do for themselves, not for us. It is why we ask all teachers at SLA to always incorporate the core values into their planning; why we all use *Understanding by Design* by Grant Wiggins and Jay McTigue (see #41) to plan our units, why we all use the

same rubric to grade all our projects. When we speak the same language about the way we teach and learn, kids can get down to the work of learning more quickly.

2 Treat your class as a lens, not a silo. The goal is for our kids to be well-rounded, thoughtful citizens. Remember that if you're lucky, 10 percent of the kids in your class will major in your subject. Make sure the other 90 percent understand how what they are learning with you helps them to be a better person.

1 Remember that we teach students before we teach subjects. We ask that all SLA teachers understand and live the profound difference between the statements, "I teach history" and "I teach kids history." Children should never be the implied object of their own education.

And one more—be kind. Be kind to your students, to your colleagues, even to your principal. Whatever you do, be kind.

From Theory to Practice

- Write your list. What are the ten or three or twenty things you ask of teachers or students on a regular basis? Write them down as a reminder of what you stand for and what you ask of others.

- Ask for the right things. That list of ten or three or twenty—does it align with the mission, vision, and values you espouse in welcome letters, school documents, class guidelines? Take time to make sure the things you ask of people reflect the kind of person, teachers, and leader you want to be. If you're more hung up on putting up learning objectives on teacher boards than you're asking about actual learning, perhaps you need to make a shift.

- Ask others what they perceive to be your top requests. There are the things we say and there are the things we *think* we say. Find the students, teachers, and administrators who know you best and whom you trust and ask them what they hear you saying and asking for the most. It's a helpful reality check.

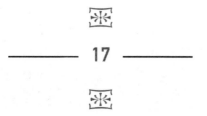

Schools Are Where We Come Together

There are those in the educational and political landscape these days who would dismantle the entire institution of school, and others who would use the tools of blended learning, technology, authentic learning experiences, and self-guided inquiry to argue that school is irrelevant. It can be a seductive argument, especially when so many schools frustrate us with the degree to which they underserve children. However, the fundamental purpose of public school—physical spaces dedicated to and people committed to educating a nation—is a good one.

There's no question that *how* we conceive of schools must change, but *why* we have them remains as vital today as it ever has been. In an age when segmentation of society keeps people apart from those who think, look, and live differently from how they do, schools bring us together to learn from and with one another.

There is a subtle and yet vital difference between the fundamental role of school in the past and its role in the modern world. For the past one hundred years, in most American schools, the school was important because it was where the information was—it was where the teacher was. The classroom was important because it was where people came together to get the information from the teacher. And while this is an oversimplification of the pedagogy of the past one hundred years, it is, sadly, an accurate description of the dominant paradigm in American education. It is the Prussian model that Horace Mann brought back from Europe and instituted across the country with great success.

And let's be clear: this model educated a nation with greater success than the world had ever seen, so we can understand why it has been so hard to let go of the old vision of what schools look like. Much of what we see in the "No Excuses" charter school model, Common Core, No Child Left Behind, and other current "reform" movements seems like an attempt to recapture the hazily remembered nostalgic days when students sat and patiently absorbed information from caring teachers. But to quote Billy Joel, "The good old days weren't always good/And tomorrow ain't as bad as it seems."[13]

So if the reason to come together in a classroom isn't because the teacher is there to dispense the knowledge, why come together in a classroom?

Because that's where we come together to learn.

A vibrant classroom filled with active learning is a wonderful place that deserves to be nurtured. Learning can happen in many ways, and not all moments of learning have to be social, but equally, not all learning moments should be solitary either. All over the world, there are classrooms where students learn together with caring, dedicated teachers. In these places, the social learning means that the whole is greater than the sum of its parts. It is the promise of these classrooms, these schools, that we must hold onto—and they are not as rare we think.

In every school, there are teachers who make the classroom someplace special. They listen to students, push them to reach beyond what they knew their grasp could be. There are students who look forward to those classes so that they can be in deep learning environments. And in all those places, the learning goes far beyond acquisition of knowledge and skills and content. In all those places, there is meaning and wisdom and passion.

And at schools like High Tech High[14] in San Diego, California, and MET Center[15] in Providence, Rhode Island, and Science Leadership Academy—to name a few—students and teachers and administrators have come together to build entire communities that learn this way. And there are many, many more schools that have built powerful learning communities out there. We just have to do a better job of identifying them and celebrating what they are doing right.

That is what school can be. As a nation, we can imagine many different models for school, but the fundamental idea that we build places where all children can come together to learn remains one of the best ideas we've ever had as a society.

We shouldn't lose it. We just have to make sure our schools reflect the time in which we live.

From Theory to Practice

- Ask yourself this question every day: "How can we leverage the wisdom, ideas, and passion of the room?" Find ways to make learning more communal so that there is a reason for that group of people to be in the room together. And then leverage tools such as Google Apps and learning management systems like Canvas to enable the idea of "coming together" to encompass more than just physical space.

- Redefine engagement. It's a curious thing when principals sit down to teacher reviews and pronounce that a certain percentage of students in an observed class were engaged. What they really mean is that percentage of students was engaged in what the teacher was saying. This is a throwback to the teacher-centric model. When people come together to learn in different ways, engagement is going to look different. Sit with your team, department, school, and so on and ask, what will learning look like if we are meeting the needs and curiosities of both the individuals and the group of students in our classes? Then decide to look for that.

- Tell the story. The same tools and affordances we encourage students to use to share their learning are at the disposal of teachers and administrators. Start a blog. Jump into an #edchat on Twitter. Attend an EdCamp. Whatever method you choose, start telling the story of the good things that are happening as people come together to teach and learn alongside one another in our schools.

⸎

———— 18 ————

⸎

What We Want for Students, We Must Want for Teachers

A friend of ours, a classroom teacher with more than fifteen years of experience working with students at all grade levels, found herself in a new school in a new city after years in another school system. Because of tough economic conditions, few teaching positions were open, and she took a job at a school about which she'd heard mixed reviews.

A few months later, she resigned from the school. She left broken in places no teacher should be broken by a school.

She left because this school, which professed great love and care for the success of students, had less of a focus, if any, on the success and care of its teachers. We can try this approach for a while, but ultimately it is unsustainable.

At her school, our friend was constantly being evaluated and given feedback that she had not met the expectations on the school-wide evaluation form. During one observation, when a student spoke out, rather than awarding that student with a demerit as policy dictated, this teacher approached the student and spoke to him as a person about community and what it means to be a member.

At the end of the lesson, the teacher's administrator commented that she'd failed to follow school protocol and so would be marked "unsatisfactory."

This is a story of a particular time and place, but it could easily be the story of innumerable schools across the country. We are treating our teachers, practicing professionals, as though they step into the classroom devoid of wisdom, caring, and creativity.

We must stop this. Teachers must refuse to subject themselves to this kind of treatment. When teachers are not trusted or allowed to connect with their students in human ways that help to model how to be members of a community, when they are forced to award consequences devoid of conversation, when their professionalism is called into question because they treat children as people, it diminishes our democracy as well as the professionalism of teachers.

In many cases, it is our youngest teachers (often with minimal training) who find themselves in these schools. As it is their first foray into professional teaching, they may not know they are justified in feeling insulted by the feedback they receive. Indeed, because of the feeling of treading water that comes with any novice teachers, they may welcome the feedback as the only chance to improve.

In time they may become dependent on this feedback, relying on the outside judgment of others in place of developing their own sense of success based on their professional opinion. Worse yet, some may master the criteria of the observation form, receive "outstanding" ratings in all areas, and come to think of this as a mark of completion. For those teachers who were the most "schooly" of students (learning to play the game of traditional school early and winning throughout their formal education), counting the approval of their assessors as success will make perfect sense.

We must want more for teachers. We must want more for teachers because we want more for students and for society.

Those who call for the improvement of the teaching profession often employ the same deficit model of thinking to the teachers they're attempting to "improve" that they apply to rhetoric about students who come from communities in poverty.

We are reminded of the passage in Eric Schlosser's *Fast Food Nation* where he describes fast food's attempt to alter production lines so that workers with no experience and limited or no English proficiency can prepare food based on a system of pictures.

While the school reform movement hasn't taken things this far, such a prospect is not as distant as some might think. Scripted curricula, check-off observation forms—these tools and others like them not only generate a stifling "one size fits all" mind-set about schools but also ask less and less of our teachers—not more.

And we should ask more of our teachers—more creativity, more imagination, more inquiry, more investigation.

As things stand, though, we are asking for more of the wrong thing—conformity—as though our children come from one mold, as though our teachers should as well.

From Theory to Practice

- Ask for the treatment you deserve. As a teacher, if your district requires a generic observation form to be filled out by your principal, sit down and ask before the observation that you also receive feedback in a form you'd prefer. This could be an extended conversation over a planning period. Or maybe you and your principal write narratives of how you thought the lesson went and then meet and compare. Whatever the preference, ask for the kind of feedback from which you can most benefit.

- Choose schools in which you believe, and work there. Our friend struggled with whether to leave the place that was breaking her. Such a move meant uncertainty for her family. In the end, she realized she was worth the move, and that she could not be part of perpetuating a system she found toxic to children and adults. Vote with your feet for the kinds of schools you want to be available to teachers.

- Shift culture from the inside. While the principal is a driving force for school culture, she isn't the only force. If you want to work in a place where the adults are cared for, where creativity is valued, where data come from multiple sources that have nothing to do with tests, then you will need to help that culture grow. Keep a collection of note cards in your room. When you hear students saying how much they appreciate a colleague's class, jot a note to that person to let them know they made a difference that crossed classrooms. If you know a colleague is doing something particularly wonderful, ask if you can sit in on class to gather ideas.

——— **19** ———

⌖

Embrace Your Best Teacher-Self

Chris started teaching when he was twenty-five years old. He taught in a school where teachers chose whether to use their first name or their last name. Some of the teachers he learned from pushed him to go by "Chris," not "Mr. Lehmann." But Chris was young (and young-looking) enough to worry about the lack of distance between himself and the eighteen-year-olds he was teaching that he wanted the daily reminder that he was the teacher in the room.

The "Mr. Lehmann" was and is often shortened to "Lehmann" or even "Lehms" or for some kids "Coach," but that person became who Chris is—or at least who he aspires to be. And the important thing is, that is who the kids need him to be.

If students are willing to see us as the kind of teachers that students believe in—that students want to be around, want to learn from—then don't we have an obligation to strive to be that person? If the students need to believe in a "Mr. Lehmann" who is far smarter, far more patient, far more humble, far more thoughtful than who Chris really is, maybe he can get closer to being that person because of their vision.

So perhaps our teacher-selves should be the best versions of who we are. On some level, our teacher-selves should be the ideal that we strive for every day, even when we know that most days we will fall far short of that ideal. That ideal of the teacher-self should keep us growing and learning as teachers. Knowing that, most days, we fall short of the best version of ourselves is the thing that should keep us profoundly humble. But we should always remember that tomorrow is another day, another chance to be the person that the students need us to be.

There's no question that, as teachers, knowing who our students are, knowing what they need, is an inquiry project that will keep us learning every day of our teaching lives, but the ancillary benefit is that knowing who we need to be in the classroom will keep us growing every day too.

Kurt Vonnegut wrote, "We are what we pretend to be, so we must be careful about what we pretend to be."[16] If we pretend to be more thoughtful, more wise, more passionate, and more kind than we actually are, and the kids help us to become those things, isn't that a good thing?

Years ago, we started pretending to be "Mr. Lehmann" and "Mr. Chase." Every day, we give what we have that day to live up to their ever-changing ideals.

From Theory to Practice

- Journal. It doesn't matter where, but it matters that you find some space to document who you were on this day or that day. It can be a public blog, a file stored on your computer, a notebook you keep in your back pocket. Whatever the method, keep track of who you were and wanted to be as you taught. Turning back to those moments will help you remember who your students need you to be.

- Start each year with a statement of purpose. When Zac was preparing to be a teacher, his professors asked him to write a simple paper titled, "Why I Want to Teach." At the conclusion of his program, he was asked to do the same assignment again and compare the two papers. It's a practice he continues to this day. At the start of your school year, sit down and write the reason you do what you do. At the end of the school year, do the same and then look at who those two people turned out to be.

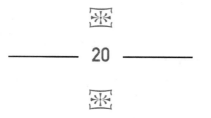

We Must Be Our Whole Selves

Remember when you were in school and saw a teacher out in the real world? Do you remember that feeling of awe as you realized this person existed outside of the classroom? It was a mind-bending experience for Zac, filled with questions—Could they still grade without the classroom? Were they talking to everyone in the grocery store about the quadratic formula? Were they hiding our homework in their purses?

Then, when we were safely back in our roles as teachers and students in the classroom, we could say, "I saw you this weekend!" as though we'd caught them out of bounds. Those are times burned into memory. Those times also have no place in the schools we need.

As much as we can, we must be our whole selves in the classroom.

It is easy to step into a classroom and decide, "This is my teacher-self. This is who the students will see." Then, when the day is done, we return to our nerdy appreciation of *Buffy the Vampire Slayer*, meet up with our kickball teams, or join with our fiction writers' workshop as though the two identities were completely separate.

The separation of our professional selves and our private selves must be maintained, to be sure. Taking the problems and worries of every student home with us each night creates martyrs, not teachers. Bringing our quarrels with partners, struggles with finances, and all the rest of it into the classroom can also take learning off track.

Still, there is a place for our whole selves in the classroom, and this is the support our students need. We bring social capital with us, and to ignore that hurts students and limits their access to the "real world."

Whatever we were before we were teachers, we must take these roles with us into the classroom. In fact, we cannot help doing so, so we might as well make it explicit.

No matter the social standing of our students outside of school, we must consider ourselves as conduits to the cultures they might come across when they leave us. Much has been made of the "funds of knowledge"[17] in which our students exist outside of schools, in their daily cultures. Teachers should and must learn from these cultures if they hope to be in and of the neighborhoods and communities in which they teach.

To that end, little to nothing has been mentioned of the funds of knowledge existing in the nonschool lives of teachers. Learning lives there. Whatever can be used by students to access the lives of their teachers can be used by teachers to access the lives of students.

As much as we must be our best teacher-selves, we must consider how much of our whole selves we can be in the classroom.

A former student recently asked about how much she might share with her students regarding her past. Now in college and preparing for student teaching, this student knew that the hardships she'd been through in childhood could act as anchors for her students. She knew she would have found it easier to navigate the difficult and tumultuous psychological spaces she had encountered if she'd had a teacher in her life who'd said, "I've been where you are, and I found the way out." Realizing she was about to enter the lives of her own students, this young woman wanted to make sure she was as transparent as she could be so that her students would see her as a source of strength if they were working through some of the same personal crises.

Teaching does not require we lay our lives bare for our students in hopes such nakedness of spirit will help them learn from our experience. It does not mean that we have to share every pain and tragedy of our lives as teachers—in fact, that could lead down a dangerous path in the classroom, shifting the focus from connecting with our students to mining our pain to make our students feel sorry for us. When possible, though, whether it means sharing a favorite television show or reliving a traumatic event, being our whole selves in the classroom gives students access not only to who we are as people, but also to who they might become.

From Theory to Practice

- Talk about pop culture. If there's a song that's been trapped in your brain for hours, play it in class, and explain that you're trying to "get it out." If there's a show you're looking forward to, share that. If you a have just finished a great book, recommend it. And ask the same of your students.

- Be more than a particular college graduate. There's a strangely pervasive trend in schools for teachers to deck out their classrooms with the memorabilia of their alma maters. While there's nothing wrong with school pride, it isn't entirely truthful to present this as the crowning achievement of our lives. One former colleague constantly told her students that they would need what she was teaching them when they found themselves in college.

Daily, she also told her fellow teachers that the students weren't showing much interest in the class. This teacher was also a former Olympian with a profoundly interesting professional history aside from teaching. Instead of sharing those experiences, she insisted on presenting college entrance as the primary drive of education. It was to her detriment and will be to your students' as well, if you do not acknowledge that all of life is the goal of living.

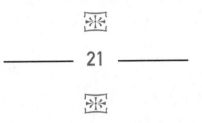

Technology Should Transform School, Not Supplant It

Technology is not a neutral tool. It is rewriting the way we think about everything in our society, from communication to security to commerce to privacy to learning. The potential for that to be a force for good is near limitless, but we should be thoughtful and even skeptical about the uses of educational technology, especially when it comes to the larger issue of school reform and the continued rise of edu-business.

In the spring of 2012, at the opening keynote of the Education Innovation Summit, Michael Moe told a room full of education entrepreneurs that over 90 percent of the many billions of dollars spent on education in the United States was spent on personnel, and the only way to further monetize the education sector, as he called it, was to reduce personnel costs.[18] To the few teachers in the room, his point was clear—if you want to use technology to make money in education, you have to find a way to reduce the number of teachers. And there are many powerful people who seem to agree with Moe's statements.

So let us be clear—technology should not be used to supplant teachers. Not ever. When we use the tools we love as an excuse to reduce the number of caring adults who interact with children, we run the risk of doing irreparable harm. In fact, we all but guarantee it.

School is about much more than Newton's laws of motion or the difference between the Articles of Confederation and the Constitution, though these things are important. When done well, schools help children learn how to live lives of meaning. When done right, schools help children become profoundly active citizens. When done with care, schools help children learn how to care for one another. Technology alone cannot do those things. The purpose of school is not to train children but to teach them, and that requires the human element. If anything, we need more adults in schools, not fewer.

Technology is and must be a transformative element in our schools. Fundamentally, it changes the equation of why we come to school. Whereas previously, we came to school because the teacher was there, now we come to school because we are all there together. Technology can allow us to embrace a more finely honed sense of community in our schools.

It's a mistake to think that we no longer need this thing called school because we have all of these new technologies. And an even greater mistake to think that all we need to do is develop the right app or the right product and we can buy and sell our way to a technological future of learning that no longer needs the people. The logical end of that path is a level of solipsism that our society cannot and should not abide.

It is not that technology should supplant school, rather that it should transform it. The promise of educational technology is that we can reinvent and reimagine schools as the center of a community of learning. It is true that we no longer have to define school as four walls and floor, but let us not use that as an excuse to throw away all that we have learned over the past hundred years of the public school experiment. Let us instead mine the rich vein of educational history to find those moments of empowerment, those moments of connection, of authenticity, of care. Let us realize that those moments—more often than not—happened at the intersection of a caring teacher and the students who trusted her. And then let us ask ourselves: how can technology enhance, magnify, multiply, and transform those moments so that more children can feel that their learning matters and that their school matters every day?

That is the promise of these tools we love so much. Anything short of a vision of educational technology use that allows students and teachers to inquire more deeply, research more broadly, connect more intensely, share more widely, and create more powerfully, sells short the power of these tools—and more important, sells short the promise of learning and of school for our students.

From Theory to Practice

- Stick to your mission and vision. If a technology wraps you in its promise of an easier teaching day, increased student results, or some other marketing ploy, ask yourself what kind of people students and teachers will become as a result of using the technology. If it's aligned with your mission and vision for the people in your care, move forward. If it's not, move away. The third option is the neutral response. If a technology looks like it will move your school neither toward or away from your vision and mission, be skeptical. Ask: What would need to happen for it to work at cross purposes? What would need to happen to ensure that it was supporting your purposes? Can you make that happen?

- Solve problems, don't start them. If a technology you're considering strikes you or someone at your school as a solution looking for a problem, then chances are you can pass on that one. You and the folks with whom you work are only human, and bringing on something that isn't solving a known and existing problem is going to draw on human resources you could probably use to greater effectiveness elsewhere.

- Celebrate the people. We often see schools whose leaders are quick to point to some technology that has "completely transformed" a math class. Our questions: "Who brought it in?" and "Who is implementing it?" The teachers in your building who are able to see transformative uses of technology deserve more praise than the technology itself. By praising those teachers publicly, you give other thoughtful and ingenious teachers permission to try to solve problems in new ways as well.

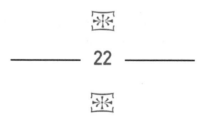

22

Build Your Own Faculty Lounge

A group of student teachers sit around a table in a classroom long after the school day has ended. They are participating in a seminar required of them by their university. The intent is to help them through student teaching. Still near the start of the semester, they're not yet in the tall grass of the student teaching experience.

"I'm just not clear on why," one of them says to their supervisor. "I mean, I don't know why Twitter would be important to teachers. What's the point?"

It's a fair question, considering each of the student teachers has just been asked to sign up for a Twitter account and assigned to participate in #engchat, one of the many weekly Twitter meetups of teachers from around the world dedicated to generating conversation and sharing resources specific to the discipline of teaching students English Language Arts.

It's a fair question not only for these student teachers, but also for any teacher who's ever looked at Twitter or some other type of social networking tool and asked, "Why?"

Our answer to these teachers: "You can't control who teaches next to you."

Though seemingly flippant, there's a serious point behind this statement.

Where faculty is concerned, only a small percentage of our school culture is within our own individual loci of control. We may sit on interview committees or help to recruit talented teachers into our schools. For the most part, though, the grim reality is that many teachers may not connect with or be inspired by the other teachers with whom we work.

Social networking tools allow for the construction of the faculty lounges we wish we had. For most people outside of schools, the teachers' lounge remains a mythical place where teachers retreat during lunch or planning and then return to class with no hint of what they've done in the interim.

For those who work in schools, we know what depressing, pessimistic places faculty lounges can be. All it takes is one teacher who's been in the classroom past his expiration date to turn an otherwise reflective space into the physical equivalent of anonymous online commenting.

Social networking tools allow teachers to escape those physical spaces and curate networks of colleagues from across the world to help improve practice, augment resources, and build conduits of collaboration. In their book, *Student Achievement through Staff Development*,[19] Bruce Joyce and Beverly Showers argue that moving from a situation of practicing theory with low-risk feedback to one of coaching, study teams, or peer feedback increases the incidence of application and problem solving in teacher practice from 10–15 percent saturation to 85–90 percent saturation. In other words, when teachers are surrounded by teams and colleagues, they are more likely to take what they are learning and put it into practice with their students. It turns out, we learn better together.

The issue? Not every teacher finds herself surrounded by peers to whom she can turn for coaching and the like. This is where the digital network should come in. Through connections with other like-minded teachers and those teachers who act as the loyal opposition, teachers can build networks of professional development while working at schools that would otherwise let their learning languish.

These are networks of people who can improve spirits on an otherwise dreary teaching day, work collaboratively in a document to help build a unit plan, and share links to the perfect resources for helping students access learning.

While there are no set ways for developing online faculty lounges, some approaches have been anecdotally helpful in building networks of support.

1. Begin by reading. The Internet has no shortage of teachers offering their thoughts on everything from education policy to professional practice. Many of those new to online networks take solace in knowing they can lurk and read long before they ever begin to craft their online selves into existence.

2. Comment. Some of the best conversation that can come from connecting via social networks is not the

production of new content, but the questioning and commenting on the work of others. This is by no means an encouragement to recklessly argue. It is more of a push in the direction of creation. If you're reading, you might as well stop and comment, right?

3. Follow the bread crumbs. While linking online can lead to an echo chamber at times, it more often can be counted on to help introduce you to new voices. In the physical world, this is the equivalent of meeting a friend of a friend and finding out you've got similar interests. One of the great benefits of hypertextual writing is that you are reading along with the writer and able to trace many of the ideas that influenced what she is saying and the ideas that influenced those ideas.

4. Embrace the fire hose. This may be the most difficult. If you were to look at the listing of online voices we follow at this moment, you'd find hundreds of posts we've not yet had the time to attend to. In traditional texts, this would be frustrating. Online, it need not be. There will always be a fire hose of information waiting for you to put yourself in front of it. Some days, you'll have time. Other times, you'll step aside and mark everything as read. That's okay. In the same way you have the right to put down a book without reaching its end, you have the right not to read everything on the Internet. No one is expecting you to. Read what you want. The rest will always be there if you change your mind.

5. Make your own path. You were likely taught to approach a book in a certain way, to look for certain markers and to take note of certain things. This need not be the case in online spaces and in curating your online networks. Let your love of learning mingle with your love of pictures of kittens. Sometimes, those posting the kitten photos are the ones who can challenge your ideas about what it means to learn in new and powerful ways.

While these are five ways to approach building your online faculty lounge, they are just as easily five ways not to build that lounge. This is the democracy of online spaces, and it is key as a contrast to the physical space where you may find yourself. You have control over those to whom you turn for support and advice, and you can always move away from those who bring pessimism to your practice.

From Theory to Practice

- For blogs, we recommend John Spencer (http://www .educationrethink.com/), Dean Shareski (ideasand thoughts.org), José Vilson (thejosevilson.com), Diana Laufenberg (laufenberg.wordpress.com), and Larissa Pahomov (lpahomov.wordpress.com). This is a tiny smattering of the thousands upon thousands of education blogs worthy of your time. Give yourself some time, follow the breadcrumbs from these, and you're bound to find the right mix.

- Communities also abound. Connecting with educators on networks such as connectedclassrooms.withgoogle.com on Google+ are a way to dive into the stream of quality conversations and resources. Social networks such as the Making Curriculum Pop (mcpopmb.ning.com) Ning group are also easy to find and join.

- Ask questions. In addition to the resources and recommendations outlined here, asking questions in any of these environments is one of the best ways to make them relevant. We must advocate for our own learning the way we hope our students will.

———— 23 ————

Don't Admire the Problem

Put any group of teachers in a room, present them with a new initiative to be introduced in their school, and ask them to come up with ten reasons why the initiative will not work. In five minutes or less, your list will be complete.

What's more, they will agree on the list. Even those who did not contribute will nod their heads with approval. This is one of those rare moments where the pedagogical stars align and everyone in a school agrees! They agree, "There's no way we can do this."

It's what our friend Kristen Hokanson describes as admiring the problem, and at schools, the practice can be studied as an art.

The solution is simple: decide not to admire the problem anymore.

At one conference, the assembled participants were interested in quick-fix solutions to integrating technology into their classroom practice. Their further intent was to move that integration into their larger school environment.

Though they shared the same goal, the only thing they could all agree on was the beauty of the problems standing in their way.

If the session had any hope of moving them forward, they needed to stop with their admiration.

To start things out, our friends and colleagues Marcie Hull and Tim Best invited participants to throw out every conceivable reason that they weren't going to be able to do what they wanted. The screen in front of them quickly was full. Marcie and Tim then asked participants if any other reasons had not been included. A few stragglers were added, and the session moved forward.

"OK," we told the participants, "we could probably admire these problems for the entire session, but we wouldn't get anywhere. So, let's take all of these as givens, and also decide that we're going to accomplish our goals anyway."

The crowd giggled nervously, and it started to work. As the workshop progressed, the list was ever present. We never ignored the problems, but we never admired them either.

Every once in a while, someone would start to slip into the reasons a given idea might not work, and a colleague would warn, "I think you're admiring the problem." The work would get back on track.

This approach, or some variant of it, is key for any school or educational system hoping to move past the problems standing in the way of positive change for the adults and students it serves. There are no perfect ideas, so therefore we can always find reasons not to enact change. As we wrote in an earlier thesis, we can acknowledge that there are no perfect ideas in education, and while we encourage everyone to examine the limitations of every idea so that the problems will be anticipated and mitigated, too often we use the inherent problems of any idea as a reason not to act. We cannot afford ourselves that luxury.

Instead, make solving the problems the focus of the process. This approach avoids admiring the problem and acknowledges that a group of dedicated professionals, through their combined experience and expertise, are capable of developing tremendous solutions.

Whatever the approach, naming the problem and declaring a moratorium on its admiration can lead to an empowered community, more open communication, and a much clearer path to positive change.

From Theory to Practice

- At your next faculty meeting where a new idea is presented, allow teachers to work through the process just described, giving faculties the chance to air their doubts and frustrations. If you don't ask, they'll be doing this anyway under their breath. The difference here is the naming of the thing at the outset. Acknowledging that a task will be difficult can keep that difficulty from becoming overwhelming down the road.

- In smaller groups like teaching teams, pausing to review each quarter and listing the hardships of the previous quarter can provide a great basis for setting goals and keeping in mind the work to be done. Perhaps the team prioritizes its roadblocks and decides to focus for a quarter on the one or two that most hinder student learning and professional development.

- Do this with students as well. Give them a chance to do this the next time you assign a project. Give them the chance to do this midway through the year. Let people see the problems, name them, and then begin working on solutions.

—— **24** ——

⌗

Not "Yeah, but—"; Instead, "Yes, *and ... "*

Building things is difficult. Building things with others, even more so. Nowhere is this more pronounced than in a conference presentation. Professionals assemble in a poorly lit room with mean, uncomfortable chairs, ostensibly to learn, grow, and take new ideas back to their home bases.

Ask those assembled to begin by turning to those around them and sharing their names, titles, and locations of origin, and you're on the right track. You'll get no argument when you ask for a few volunteers to share what's wrong, broken, or difficult about the systems in which they work.

This becomes admiring the problem again. If allowed to roam free, it's likely an entire conference session could be dedicated to admiring the problem. If conference sessions don't fit your context, imagine a faculty lounge at lunch break, a faculty meeting, a learning community meeting—just about any place professionals meet, it's likely they can fill every nook and cranny of the space with admiration of the problem.

Ask them to take a moment to consider a possible solution to that problem, though, and the mood will change. Or to be precise, the mood will stay the same and the solution will be sentenced to death by a chorus of "Yeah, but—."

No matter the research, evidence, data, and testimonials behind a solution, the cries of "Yeah, but—" will tumble out of mouths in an avalanche of negativity.

We are no longer simply admiring the problem; now we've fallen in love with it.

In the schools we need, we must take a stance of "Yes, *and* ... "

"Yes, and ... " is the fundamental principle of improvisational theater. When no lines, no script, and no direction are driving a scene, actors must trust that their scene partners will accept what they say and do and immediately build off of it.

Imagine the power of such a mind-set when someone presents an assembled audience with a teaching practice that has opened up learning for her students. Instead of "Yeah, but that would never work for our kids because ... " the answer becomes, "Yes, and here are the ways we'd need to tweak what you're talking about for it to fit our scenario."

Do not misunderstand—"Yes, and ... " does not avoid conflict. Instead, it embraces conflict and builds from the difficulties rather than seeing the problem as the conclusion.

Another way to think about this is in the shape of the "barn raising" approach described by Don McCormick and Michael Kahn.[20] Pointing out the stonewalling that can often take place in a college seminar discussion where all voices are attempting to be heard—stonewalling by means of either ignoring or tearing down those ideas that come before them—McCormick and Kahn suggest another approach, with these four suggestions:

1. The classroom battle is not a good way to teach thinking.

2. Even if it were, it makes idea-conversation so unpleasant that students do their best to avoid it, in college and afterward.

3. The classroom battle is a significant contribution to the building of a society of contention and enmity.

4. And, as an alternative, there is another way to talk
   about ideas, one that obviates those difficulties.

McCormick and Kahn use the metaphor of a barn raising, in
which all parties are working to build something new and useful
to the group. While each may have a different skill or task to complete, they are working toward a common cause of creation rather
than destruction or limitation of the others. To be successful, all
must be successful.

Both "Yes, and … " and barn raising take reality as their foundations. Both acknowledge the present situation or problem as
the starting point for any work to be done. They find their usefulness in refusing to stand around and take into account all the
factors that make finding a solution so difficult. "This is the reality," these approaches say, "and now we will work together to build
a new and better reality."

From Theory to Practice

- Pay attention to your habits. In the next meeting you
  attend, keep a sticky note in front of you and make a
  tick mark each time you say or want to say something
  that explains why a given idea is bad or won't work.

- Once you've got an idea of where your "Yeah, buts" lie, set a
  goal of agreement. While it's tempting to begin with a trial
  of twenty-four hours of trying to build barns, changing
  habits is more difficult than that. Try one class period of
  agreeing with and building ideas with your students. Increase
  from there.

- Set time aside for agreement in whichever groups you're
  responsible for. If you've got a classroom of students,
  explain that you're going to throw out an idea, and
  it's everyone's responsibility to accept the idea and
  build upon it with the fundamental idea of "How

could I help this idea work?" If you're in charge of a faculty meeting, apply the same idea in that space. Agreement is a muscle that must be built over time.

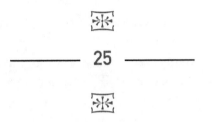

Ignore the Seat Back

The man sits asleep in his window seat, mouth agape. The flight attendant reaches over and gingerly taps him on the shoulder.

"Sir," he says, "we'll be landing soon, and I need you to put your seat up."

"I can't," says the passenger. "Whenever I try, it just falls back down. I think it's broken."

"You need to press the button."

"I did. It just keeps falling back." He demonstrates.

"Well, see if you can put up the seat next you," the flight attendant says, and walks away.

The passenger is suggesting someone might want to report the broken seat, but the flight attendant has already moved on.

The entire scene is reminiscent of many teachers' approach to students and what they have decided are the correct behaviors.

Anyone who has ever traveled by air knows the vehemence with which flight attendants insist passengers put their seat backs and tray tables in the fully upright and locked position.

So too might anyone who observes an American classroom note the force with which many teachers insist students follow exacting classroom procedures and practices. Students must submit their homework at a given time, tests must be completed within a certain interval, essays must be formatted according to set parameters. In many cases, if any of these standards is not met, the work will not be accepted. The students will not be cleared for landing.

Teachers are tripping over procedures with little regard for their intended destinations.

Certainly, it is important for a student to learn the lesson of submitting work in a timely manner. At the same time, the tardiness of work should not mean a student's effort up to that point should be disregarded.

Why, then, do many teachers impose such draconian measures in their classrooms? They do it for the same reasons many flight attendants insist on upright seats—not because it is imperative for the landing of the plane, but because it is one of the few things still within their control.

If teaching is entirely dependent on others' listening and observing instruction and then internalizing it, it is little wonder that teachers might savor any element of control they can find when faced with the lackluster success rates of much traditional teaching.

One option, the option of which we are fervent proponents, is to keep the intended destination in mind when responding to the idiosyncrasies of student behaviors and accepting successes while working to improve upon failures. This is not easy.

Our flight attendant, too, struggled with keeping the destination in mind. If seat back position were important to the operation of the plane, he would have done well to listen to the passenger and report the defunct chair. Ignoring it now means he and subsequent flight attendants will wage a constant battle with that seat when a few moments of focused attention could spare them all that frustration.

Teachers too could learn from this piece of the story. Punishing the student who has formatted his essay incorrectly, without taking the time to help the student develop a plan for avoiding the error in the future, only ensures headaches down the road.

Failing to appreciate the work that's been done or to work toward a solution while simultaneously punishing the annoyance leads to something we've mentioned before at which educators are particularly adept—admiring the problem.

From Theory to Practice

- Know why, and know when there's no why. If you are particularly persnickety about a deadline, ask yourself why that happens to be. If somewhere in your curriculum it says you must teach your students to adhere to exacting deadlines, it's understandable to ask that of them from time to time. If the essay or problem set they're handing in was designed to help you understand their development in other skills, perhaps the few students who got theirs to you a bit late will not become the criminals and hooligans you take their tardiness to suggest.

- Remember the real "real world." Often teachers will insist on the raising of educational seat backs, citing the real world's lack of tolerance for missed deadlines, talking in the hallways, using cell phones, and so on. We worry many of these teachers haven't seen the real world. Yes, there are times when these things need special attention, but we would be hard-pressed to make a case for paying attention to them all the time. There is real learning to be done and real problems to be solved in the real world. Perhaps focusing on that would lead to the other elements solving themselves.

- If you outlaw something, reconsider it, and try unofficially ignoring its presence in your learning space for a week. If the walls are still up after a few days, think about what that might say about the practices to which you cling.

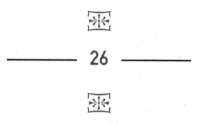

Find Meaning Every Day

When Chris was first out of college, he lived in Washington, D.C., and part of his daily walk to work took him past the Capitol building. When he first started, he was awed by what it meant to walk past that building, but it quickly became his routine, and most days he barely even noticed it. The same was true for Zac when he moved to the Gulf Coast of Florida for his first teaching job. The beaches and sunsets were amazing for the Illinois transplant. With time, though, the beaches and the sunsets became the stops that were made to impress visiting guests, rather than places and times for wonder and reflection.

It's inevitable that even the most amazing of environments becomes routine, and when it does, it becomes easy to lose sight of what makes it so special in the first place.

This can be true of the most incredible schools as well. In the end, no matter how empowering, no matter how amazing, no matter how meaningful the work is, there are going to be days when the work feels like, well, work. And the most powerful learning experience can be unappreciated.

That's OK. We shouldn't fear that. If anything, we should embrace it.

We live in a world where we expect the spectacular, and more often than not, people are disappointed when the everyday lives we lead fall short of that. Schools can help us celebrate what we have that is special—and help us revalue that every day.

For both of us, it often took someone from outside the daily routine of our lives—a friend who was visiting from out of town, for example—to make us remember how special our surroundings were. At SLA, we are reminded every year, as is our entire community, of how lucky we are to be together when six hundred or so teachers from all over the country descend on us for EduCon.

On the first day of EduCon, our school becomes truly transparent. Hundreds of teachers can wander our halls, sit in on classes, take tours with students, or sit with teachers and discuss their craft. The entire weekend represents hundreds of hours of work of students, parents, and teachers to create a powerful experience for our guests. And for all of us it is a humbling moment to see so many people come to our school to learn with and from us. As SLA alum and former EduCon cochair Alaya White has said, "It makes you realize how special our school is when so many people want to know about the way we learn."[21]

But it shouldn't take an EduCon to do that. We can make the everyday meaningful in some very basic ways in every school.

From Theory to Practice

- Students and teachers should take time every day to ask of their work, "What does this hold for me? Why am I learning and teaching what I am teaching today, and what relevance does this have?" When this becomes habit, we really can train ourselves as teachers and students to make the work meaningful.

- This again is true for teachers and students alike—we can ask ourselves every day, "What did I do of value today?" And while this question may seem to be related to the preceding one—and it is—it is also important to note how it is different, because it forces us to reflect on our own actions and challenge ourselves to be of value. Those questions are harder days on some days than on others. But if we can make those questions routine in our schools, we can work together to look inward and outward as a community every day.

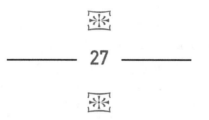

27

Take What You Do Seriously, but Don't Take Yourself Seriously

When Chris was sixteen, he and his three best friends decided to see how many tissues they could shove into their mouths. There was no reason. It was after school one day, and it was something they could compete over. Chris was "winning" this contest when the gag reflex kicked in and he came closer to choking to death than he'd like to admit.

We tell this story to say this—no matter what Chris does in his life, he is still the same moron who nearly died in a tissue-mouth-shoving contest. That's an important point.

Think of the most ridiculous thing you did in high school. You are still that person. You will always be that person. It does not matter how much wisdom you have accumulated in the intervening years, you are still that person.

And that's a good thing for so many reasons.

A career in education is a powerful way to spend your life. The work we do is important, meaningful, and incredibly challenging. We should take the work of helping children learn incredibly seriously. But we should remember to never take ourselves all that seriously. Because, to quote the kids, "It's just not that deep."

When we have the humility to remember all the twists and turns in the path that got us to where we are today, we are more likely to be understanding of the twists and turns in the paths our students take.

When we don't fall in love with our own ideas, we remain open to change and growth. We are more likely to allow our ideas to be influenced and made better by our students and our colleagues.

When we remember to laugh at ourselves, we display an openness to students that is important to model.

When we have enough sense of the long view of our lives, we laugh more easily, smile more broadly, and are more likely to share a sense of joy with the people around us.

When we are not overly invested in our own seriousness of purpose, we remember that we are the lucky ones—we get to spend our working lives teaching and learning with our students, and really, that's a pretty awesome way to spend our time.

When we don't take ourselves too seriously, we remember that the work isn't about us. It's about the kids.

So let's find a reason to laugh with the kids and our colleagues every day. Pick up the guitar and play with the kids, even if we sing off key. Play basketball with our students, even if they cream us. Let's let them see us as whole people, so that they might let us see them the same way.

And then, when we can really all talk to one another without the view of each other's egos in the way, we can ask them what they think about our schools, and we can listen deeply to their answers and let their ideas change our own.

From Theory to Practice

- Admit that you don't know. Often when we see teachers resisting technology and its integration into learning and teaching, it's because those teachers are worried about looking foolish when trying to make a new tool or digital resource do what they want it to. Admit to your students that you're lost in a problem at the front of the class and ask for help solving it. (Note: Stay away from the words, "I'm not a computer person" or any derivations thereof. You want your students to have a growth mind-set, and that can start with you modeling the fact that you're learning in all moments.)

- Laugh. Laugh easily and fully in front of your students. Tell jokes, and ask your students for them. Laughing with your students is one of the most inclusive acts you can engage in. For those who take themselves very seriously in the classroom, moving from stiff upper lip to even a chortle can be a difficult move. Set aside two to three minutes twice a week and ask your students to share whatever appropriate jokes they have, with the goal of getting you to laugh. This is a great chance to discuss appropriate humor, and it structures in some time to loosen up.

———— 28 ————

Don't Fall for Authoritarian Language

A young teacher we know in Philadelphia recently liked a teacher's post on Facebook. It was one of those posts that said something like "I am a no-nonsense teacher, here to make sure you learn," and it included the line, "My classroom is not a democracy," among other chestnuts of autocratic teacher-language.

We want this teacher—and all teachers—to be better than that.

We want her to understand that the choices she makes as a teacher will be better if she listens to students—not just the questions they ask about math or science or English, but the meta-questions they ask as well.

We want her to understand that her authority as a teacher comes not from being "tough," but rather from being caring.

We want her to understand that when we use language that denies students agency, there will be students in that classroom who will view us as more concerned with our subjects than with them, no matter how much we tell them in other moments that we care about them.

We want her to understand that, yes, we need to hold kids accountable for their work, but if we do not listen to why an assignment was missed, we may lose a moment to understand our students better.

We want her to understand that our classrooms are about the intersections of our needs and our students' needs, and that in too many classes the question "What do you need right now?" is never asked.

We want her to understand that classrooms *can* be democratic, so that students can learn how and when and why to use their voice in learning spaces—and in all spaces.

We want her to understand that posts like the one she liked are dangerously seductive. To a young teacher who doesn't feel fully at home in her teacher-self yet, the idea that we can be the authoritarian figures in our classrooms feels comforting and empowering, but the empowerment that poster was offering comes at the cost of the agency of our students.

We want her to understand that she can be a teacher who has the respect of her students, who can create smart systems and structures that allow all students to learn, who can have a classroom that is a place of powerful learning, and who can listen to students' needs at the same time. And while that might seem really daunting, especially in that first year, it is always, always worth it.

From Theory to Practice

- Read Herbert Kohl's powerful essay, "I Won't Learn from You,"[22] and ask yourself, "Am I creating spaces where kids will not learn from me because of who I present myself to be?" Examine your own practice for the moments when the conditions of learning are set only because of your decree, and ask yourself how you can achieve your goals with more student buy-in.

- Consider creating a Google-style 80 percent/20 percent policy in your class, giving students the agency to create their own projects that demonstrate their point of entry or interest for the subject of the course. Create the space for everyone to exhibit their ideas, and then be fearless in bringing student ideas back into the "real" curriculum of the class.

- Ask your students. The conversation may take some time to ease into, but it will be worth it to ask your students where they feel like they have voice and agency in their time with you, and where they would like you to you relinquish some of your more authoritarian tendencies. This is a step to take when you feel like you can process what you hear without replying in anger or defensively.

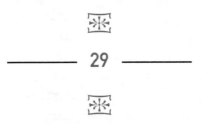

Don't Be Authoritarian—Have Authority

Listen to any group of novice teachers—those in their first few years, those student teaching, those teaching a new grade level for the first time—and you're likely to hear some variation of the following: "Yeah, most days, it's all I can do just to get control of the class." It's a question frequently asked of mentor teachers: "How do you get control of the kids?"

Lest you think such speech is solely the domain of novice teachers, try speaking at a conference session or staff development meeting and advocating a shift in practice that would mean giving students more choice in the classroom. Within seconds, a few hands will be raised, one will be called on, and a veteran teacher will say, "Yeah, that sounds great and all, but if we did what you're suggesting our classrooms would be madhouses. It'd be too difficult to keep control."

Good.

There is a difference between being an authority and being authoritarian, and we should shoot for the former.

If the bulk of teachers' practices are geared around maintaining control of the classroom or control of the students, then they've lost sight of what's possible in schools. Scott Paris and Julienne Turner give four key components of this in their piece, "Situated Motivation": choice, challenge, collaboration, and control.[23]

Sometimes we use the concept of motivation as a whitewashed way of thinking about control: "That student is really motivated," or "That teacher is very motivational." Replace "motivation" with "control" in those two sentences and you get to the meat of the meaning.

Paris and Turner found that motivation, like control, is not inherent in the individual. Anyone who has planned a lesson that turns out to be amazingly successful one day and then felt like a ringmaster the next knows this to be true. Instead, Paris and Turner found that motivation is situated in the context of an activity. It turns out that activities, not people, are motivational.

The pathway to motivational activities includes the four key components identified by Paris and Turner—choice, challenge, collaboration, and control. The more of these components a teacher builds into a learning experience, the more likely they are to find a class that might be construed as being in their control. Structuring lessons to include student choice, challenge, collaboration, and control will move the teacher to a different role than that of authoritarian. He will find himself as he should be—an authority.

The teacher as authority knows the content of the day, knows her students, knows the community, and knows how to structure a learning experience that will produce motivation in his students. This is the role of the teacher. Contrary to the tenor of much of the driving conversation about teachers, we are authorities. We are authorities of education, and we must be willing to stand up and say as much.

Sadly, it is not only the reformist/traditionalist camps that are wearing away the authority of teachers, though they are the ones whose practice tends toward authoritarianism.

Progressives have long construed the works of John Dewey to suggest that teachers should step back, hide their authority, and let students fail as they will without assistance. This is decidedly neither what Dewey meant nor what he wrote.

In his small but powerful *Experience & Education*, Dewey wrote, "On the contrary, basing education upon personal experience may mean more multiplied and more intimate contacts between the mature and the immature than ever existed in the traditional school, and consequently more, rather than less, guidance by others."[24]

What Dewey was certainly arguing against, and what does not become a great school or great community, is teacher as authoritarian, dictating actions, answers, and access with little to no regard for students' abilities to navigate those spaces on their own.

Control is a tempting mistress. In the absence of wisdom and the ability or will to structure motivating learning experiences for students, it is frequently the goal of many classroom teachers of all stripes. To build the schools we need, though, we must be authorities within a democracy.

From Theory to Practice

- Create conversation spaces within the flow of your class in which students can discuss, as a whole group, how they see the class functioning, what they'd like to see, and how they propose that things move in that direction. Ask someone to take notes during these conversations, and then return to the archive each time to see where you left things, and what was agreed upon at the close of the last talk.

- Count to ten before jumping in. In the minor moments when you know you would likely step in and "resolve" a conflict or answer students' questions, don't do it. Count to three, or ten, or whatever it takes to give students space to think things through. Often when we step in we're taking away from students the time they need to process their problems and propose solutions.

- Discover the areas of authority your students bring into your classes. Ask students what they know about and are good at, and publish that list publicly in the room. When new areas of authority are discovered or attained, pause to recognize them and add them to the list. Such a practice will reposition you as a coauthority in the space, and acknowledge the authority of students.

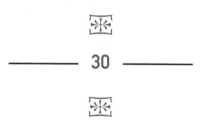

Be Silly

The requisite announcements had been completed, the student skit designed to encourage students to keep on track in the new trimester had been performed. Zac was feeling certain our community circle was about to wrap up and the students were about to head to classes.

Nope.

The sophomore with the microphone announced it was time for Crew Olympics. The couple of hundred assembled high school students took a collective moment before the crowd was peppered with the start of cheers. Our host had another announcement. The game—musical chairs. The competitors—the faculty.

At 9:45 in Codman Academy, a school that has had 100 percent of its graduates accepted to four-year colleges, the faculty who helped make that happen walked down the aisles of the meeting hall to represent their crews. In other schools, "crews" might be called "advisories," and these teachers were out to represent.

The chairs were assembled, Reel to Real's "I Like to Move It" blasted from the PA, and the teachers started circling the chairs—slowly. Painfully slowly. No one wanted to be out. Some primal preschoolian instincts were revived. Plus, they were doing it for the kids.

The first few eliminations were mundane. Expectedly, the more timid of the teachers were the first to go. They had spirit, but realized the dangers of the sport.

Things got interesting when Round Four signaled the beginning of double eliminations. By that point, those teachers who remained were in it to win it. A few went for chairs and found themselves on the floor. As they exited the arena, they were cheered, and those who remained high-fived and "good game"-ed them.

A few rounds later, there were three. Somewhere, on the other side of the hall, chanting started. Before long, little else could be heard other than the blaring of a hundred voices calling for their champions.

In that round, another fell. Literally, he ended up on the floor.

The two others who remained helped him up and shook his hand.

Somewhere in the course of the ten minutes of the game, the crowd had risen to its feet. It was impossible to watch without leaning in and selecting a personal favorite.

The music picked up somewhere in the middle of Beyoncé's "Single Ladies." The competitors—two grown, college-educated men—circled a single plastic chair. The students screamed in glee. The music played longer than it had in any other turn. On one downbeat, the contestants thought the music stopped and attempted to sit only to be cheered on by the crowd. We would see the game played out.

The taller of the two men was the first to sit. But as he was sitting back, his opponent lunged to lie flat across the seat. The judges swarmed in as the chair and the two men toppled backward.

Seconds later, the shorter man was named the winner, and first his crew, then the entire room exploded in applause.

As both men, appropriately dizzy, walked back to their seats, a retraction was made. The judge's decision was reversed.

The students were dismissed. Classes began.

The entire episode took fifteen minutes of the day. In that brief time, in this game of musical chairs, the school and its faculty had taught many lessons.

The students had seen their teachers more fully and had developed more complex understandings of who they were as people. They saw what sportsmanship could look like. While the teachers good-naturedly ribbed one another during the game, each eliminated player was sent out with a handshake or high five. Those leaving the game did so with smiles on their faces. They'd done what they'd come to do—play.

Though the teachers were representing separate crews, those separations never kept them from enjoying and supporting the whole. If all they'd been thinking of was their crews, the game could never have started.

No one processed any of this with the students. It happened, and the day moved on. As it should have. There are times to reflect and there are times for ritual. This game of musical chairs was silly, fun, and energizing. And it was ritual—an act of community to remind members who they are, of what they are a part, and how they play together.

Our students look to us to help them learn not only the academic content of our classes but also the more subtle content of navigating the world. With mandates, annual goals, and all the other seriousness incumbent upon teachers, it is frighteningly simple to forget the silly. As we've written before, we must be one school. Building on that, we must model what it means to be whole people. This game of musical chairs did just that. Students and teachers were able to see one another beyond content areas, quizzes, and homework assignments. The wall of the emotional affect was lowered, and a school was able to participate in one of the single most powerful acts of community—laughing together.

From Theory to Practice

- Resurrect Field Day. Lose a whole day to ridiculous competitions between grades and classes. Play tug-of-war, have Dizzy Bat races, and have teachers serve as coaches for the kids. Have a ridiculous trophy that gets passed down every year to the winning team. Suggest that kids make up T-shirts and get as into it as they can. Make it fun for as many people—students, teachers, and other staff—as you possibly can.

- Make music at lunch with your students. Have impromptu jam sessions with kids if you play an instrument, or just hook your iPhone up to a speaker, play the latest pop song, and sing along. It doesn't matter if you are on key—this isn't choir; the goal is just to make a joyful noise with your students.

- Read *Play* by Stuart Brown.[25] This short book makes a compelling case for the psychological, physiological, and sociological need for play in child and adult lives. Brown makes his argument based on several decades of research, and he lays out the reasons we should be working play back into schools, not forcing it out.

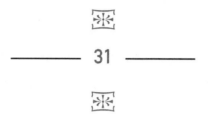

Be in the Room

In any system—you name it—there's a power structure in place. In few places is this more evident than the American public school system. Trace its roots to the British school model, or draw the parallels to the manufacturing model of the Industrial Revolution, or connect the current structure to the business innovations of the 1920s—no matter what, it's easy to overlay traditional power hierarchies on traditional schools.

Control and power rest in the hands of one person who answers to a board. The board is largely hands-off unless this manager starts to take things in the wrong direction. From there you can draw the obvious parallels between middle management, department heads, classroom teachers, and the workers on the factory floor—the students.

The power structure is in place. Except it isn't. In schools where new and vibrant ideas have a chance of flourishing, you'll find individuals or groups of individuals who didn't get the memo on the power structure. If they did, they forgot to read it.

Though we are of uncertain of its origin, one of our favorite quotations comes from an episode of *The West Wing* where Martin Sheen's President Bartlett says, "Decisions are made by those who show up."

This is a key tenet in the movement of modern schools in the direction of progress for all who teach and learn within their walls. And the best way to show up is to put yourself in the room. Wherever decisions are made at your school, be there. If there is a meeting where decisions affecting the culture of learning are being made, be there.

In many schools, in many systems, we've met people who complain they feel disempowered by the way things are done. They sit with an idea for change that could benefit the entire community, but they are waiting to be invited into the room. It's not going to happen.

Walk into any administrative space in any school and you will find adults treading water to effectively, if not efficiently, get things done. This need to take care of business often precludes any chance of pausing to look around to see if anyone is sitting in the corner with their hand raised.

Be in the room, and be ready to explain what you can do to make the school a better place. If you're not heard, put yourself in the room again. Make yours an undeniable presence wherever decisions are made. Show up so often that others find your absence strange.

It will almost certainly be uncomfortable, and success at advocating for your idea will be difficult. But, as Zac's mom always says, "If you don't ask, the answer is always no."

The flipside of this cannot be ignored by those in leadership positions. No matter how wide a principal's open-door policy, there will always be teachers and other members of the school community who cannot bring themselves to walk through the doorway.

They've been too conditioned by the system to not speak unless spoken to. These are often the teachers who were good at school when they were students. They learned to live within the hierarchy of the system. No matter the policy of willing leaders in their schools, it will take direct questioning, direct invitations, and direct listening for these teachers to truly feel welcomed in the room.

A principal interested in building a school based on community and not on hierarchies must work to model that community by actively seeking it out.

A teacher interested in contributing to the building of community in schools must make the decision to be in the room whenever possible, to pitch an idea at a moment's notice, and to be willing to revise and pitch again.

In the best schools, everyone is welcome in the room, and everyone shows up.

From Theory to Practice

- If you are a principal, make sure every teacher in your school has scheduled time with you or a member of your administrative team (if you're a big school) at least once a semester to talk about school-wide issues. Make sure that is time for the teachers to talk to you about what is on *their* minds, not what is on your mind. Keep track of ideas, and find ways to bring those ideas to other people. When ideas from these meetings are implemented, be sure to give credit where credit is due, so that more people are empowered to treat those meetings seriously.

- If you are a teacher, be prepared to "manage up." If your principal does not have a walk-in policy, or if you are not kind of person who does well with spontaneous meetings, schedule time. Be smart about how you ask for it, because most people want to know why someone wants to schedule a meeting with them. Give them a quick synopsis of the ideas you'd like to discuss. If your administrator is not responsive, leverage existing structures. Most schools have building committees or school leadership teams. Don't be afraid to use those structures to bring new ideas to the table.

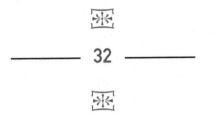

Don't Get Ego-Invested

One of our teachers came into Chris's office and said, "I'm concerned about one of my students." When Chris asked why, the teacher told him that the student had her head down in class and was really not engaging in the lesson. He went over to her and gave her some options—she could reengage with the class if she was capable, she could go see her coadvisor, go see the counselor, or even go to Chris's office and just be, but she couldn't stay in class unengaged. The student left class but didn't go any of those places, which the teacher quickly realized. He used our Slate system—the School Information System that we created with the Philadelphia web development firm Jarv.us (http://slate.is)—to send a message of concern to the student, her mom, and Chris. The student had been having a rough go of it lately, so this was not the first message that mother had received.

The young woman returned to class after being called by her mom, and as the teacher checked in with her, she looked at him and said, "Why do all you teachers have to be so [you can imagine the word she used] helpful all the time? Why can't you just leave us alone?"

The teacher didn't react in a "How dare you use that language with me?" manner. He didn't send her to the office. And he definitely did not turn the situation into a power struggle in the classroom. Instead, he saw a student whom he had known for three years as an advisee and a student who was not OK, and he saw that, in that moment, he was not going to be the adult who was able to break through her anger and get her. So he came to Chris.

Not to get her in trouble.

Not to "report" her.

But to see if Chris could help.

That matters. A lot.

So Chris found her and asked her to come to his office. Needless to say, she thought she was in trouble. Students know they shouldn't curse out their teachers.

Instead, Chris told her that her teacher was worried about her, and he asked her what we could do to help.

And the wall came down. She was having a really lousy day. Nothing earth-shattering, nothing that wouldn't get better, but the kind of day that really makes it hard to be in a classroom, because there's no way you're going to focus.

She and Chris talked about that for a while. And then Chris was able to say, "You know, you cursed out your advisor, and his first reaction was that he was worried you weren't OK. He could have gotten all teacher-angry on you, and he didn't."

That was all she needed. She said, "Yeah, that wasn't OK, what I did. I need to go talk to him. I need to go apologize. I wasn't mad at him. That wasn't right to do that."

That's massive. That's the ball game. It is everything we want.

And it happened because a teacher cared more about his student than he did about his teacher-self.

It happened because a teacher knew that it really does take a village sometimes, and he knew that it was going to take more than one adult to help the student with where she was that day.

It happened because a student was very willing to move past her own defensiveness and see that she wasn't "in trouble," but that her behavior hurt someone who cared for her, and that wasn't OK with her.

Mostly it happened because that teacher wasn't ego-invested in his dominance in the classroom. He saw pain where others might have seen only defiance. He saw a kid he cared about, a kid he knew cared about him, lashing out, and that worried him enough to ask for help.

We can get ego-invested in so many ways in our classrooms. We can fall in love with our own sense of authority. We can fall in love with our ability to be the one to "save" kids who don't need saving but who need care. We can fall in love with the bunker mentality—that we, and only we, can make a difference, to the exclusion of the other adults in a child's life.

This teacher did none of those things, so a young woman could trust him and could own her own mistake without feeling defensive. And yes, she doubled back to him and apologized completely. She owned that she was wrong, that she had treated him poorly, and that he didn't deserve it. And she simply apologized, meant it, and told him she would do better.

We are sure that she missed some good course content that day. But we trust that she can catch up. What she—and we—learned that day was every bit as important.

From Theory to Practice

- Often the conflicts between teachers and students (a) are unrelated to what is going on in school, (b) are due to a student's inability to understand something in the classroom, or (c) stem from a student's frustration with her own lack of success. Examine a recent conflict you have had with a student. Ask yourself, "What was the student really angry about?" If we can understand student anger from a different perspective, we can work with students from a very different perspective. Find the student you had that conflict with. Be willing to sit down and ask him questions about why he was angry and if there was anything you could have done differently in that moment to have defused that anger.

- Talk to other teachers. Don't assume that everything in your classroom has to happen in a vacuum. If a student is on a sports team, ask the coach how she works with the student. If a student has better success in another classroom, talk to that teacher. If everyone is frustrated, bring in another voice—a counselor or an administrator—who is willing to sit with the student and a teacher or two and talk through the frustration.

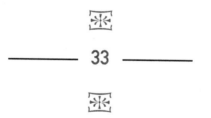

Plant Perennials

A teacher at a professional conference where Zac was speaking was proudly gushing over her current group of students. It's a wonderful thing, and we love to be near teachers who take such pride in the learning of their students. The energy that comes from those feelings is important. Students can feel the pride they inspire, and teachers are driven to find more reasons to appreciate their students' learning.

Not wanting to take away from that pride, Zac was still compelled to ask a question we frequently offer to teachers who find such pride in what they and their students are able to accomplish in a ten-month cycle.

"What is going to happen to them next year?"

As is frequently the case, the teacher took a beat.

She understood the question, but couldn't understand why he'd asked it. Here they were, appreciating the beauty of this school year—the here and now—and he'd gone and asked about the future.

"I teach eighth grade," she finally said. "So, they'll be in high school next year."

"And?" Zac asked.

Another beat.

"And I probably won't see many of them. Some of my students come back to visit," she said.

Sensing her discomfort, Zac changed the subject.

Her puzzlement over his questions was representative of the vast majority of teachers we've taken down similar lines of thinking.

"Let me enjoy my 180 days," they all seem to want to say.

By all means, enjoy your 180 days, but remember that they aren't the only 180 days a student will be in school. They aren't the only 180 days we have to help students develop questions, search for answers, and become better versions of themselves.

As David Sobel writes about his work with schools in *Place-Based Education*, "We're planting perennials, not annuals."[26]

In building the schools our children and adults need, we must turn our attention to planting perennials.

While the structures of most traditional schools make it easier to focus on the single academic year most teachers spend with a given group of students, there's no decree from on high mandating that teachers and students think and act only in such a monolithic way.

There's evidence to support the idea of teachers looping with groups of teachers through a stretch of students' school lives. Anywhere from a single teacher to an entire team begins sixth grade teaching a group of students and continues with them through middle or even high school. But such an approach would mean rebuilding the box of most schools. Such rebuilding is often vetoed as too difficult, too taxing, or too risky.

However, as is often the case, planting perennials doesn't have to require rebuilding the box; it can simply mean rethinking how we act within our current restrictions.

Our friend Darren Kuropatwa took such an approach in his math classroom. Darren was an early adopter of class blogging, and after a few years, with Darren's encouragement, his former students began returning to the blogs of his current students and commenting on their thinking, their learning, and their creativity.[27]

Although the whole of Darren's blogging approach is interesting, the connections he fostered to keep the learning relevant across generations of students planted a perennial approach to learning. Former students were able to use their knowledge in new and diverse ways to teach those who came after, while Darren's current students were exposed the next levels of work and models of the success possible as a result of the work they were doing.

Darren's approach included the use of tech tools, but planting perennials can be a low- or no-tech endeavor as well. It can be as simple as leaving your contact information in students' cumulative files in case their future teachers have questions or need a more complete portrait of the people walking into their classrooms.

Yes, we should be proud of our students and their growth within the school year. At the same time, to truly foster that growth, we must think of how we can help our students build on their growth once their season with us has passed.

From Theory to Practice

- Run an after-school activity that students come back to year after year. There's a reason that students remember coaches or the director of the school play. Often those relationships are cultivated over years. It shouldn't surprise us that those relationships are often the most important to both students and teachers.

- Create projects that don't end with the end of a marking period or a school year. Community service projects that allow students to continue with the work as they progress in high school and mentor younger students through the process are wonderful ways to build something that matters to students and to the school community.

- Write with your students over time and give them the opportunity to keep writing after they have left your classroom. Darren's math class blogs were one way to do that, but there are many other ways. Find one that makes sense for you.

——— **34** ———

⌘

Cocreate Community

"I'm glad you didn't observe me today," a teacher comments. "We lost the lesson plan for twenty minutes while we had a whole-class discussion about what language students thought was appropriate in class conversations."

That's a conversation worth observing. More important, it's a conversation well worth having. Such conversations, and other informal, unplanned interactions between and among students and teachers are the only authentic way to forge community within the classroom.

In the schools we need, community is cocreated.

Most any thoughtful teacher—novice or expert—will tell you they want their classrooms to be communities and they want their students to see themselves as community members. They have their students sitting in groups. They assign projects where students turn in work with more than one name attached to it. But these teachers are mistaking adjacency with community—thinking that students being in proximity to one another is the same thing as community formation.

Similarly, in staff development, administrators ask teachers to group together vertically, horizontally, by discipline—all in the name of forming professional learning communities. Teachers are asked to talk with each other about the work in their classrooms, discuss students, and revise lesson plans. Such actions, though, do not a community make.

Communities—at least the communities these teachers and administrators are attempting to foster—are not created by fiat. While any number of things could result in intended communities looking more like committees, there are a few conditions that are likely to allow for or even encourage community formation.

In his book *Facilitating Group Learning*, George Lakey outlines several tips for living up to the text's title.[28] Perhaps the most important and oft-forgotten is the creation of space for disagreement or argument in places of learning. He speaks to the need to understand that people coming from different ethnic and socioeconomic backgrounds are also coming from different approaches to disagreement. When there is safe space for argument, there is safe space for community to be built and for members of that community to come to understand where their voice fits within discussions and what others' voices sound like at different levels of engagement.

To assist in navigating conflict in the search for common cause is the work begun by Gordon Allport on contact theory[29] (sometimes called the contact hypothesis). The gist of the theory is that people will have less bias toward and be more connected to other groups (ethnic, gender, age, and so on) if individuals have a chance at meaningful contact with members of those other groups.

While much work has been done to expand on and examine Allport's theory in the intervening years, his original work stated that the following four components were necessary for successful communication:

1. Equal status between groups
2. Common goals
3. Intergroup cooperation
4. Authoritative support

It's easy to see some of these in place in the scenarios described earlier. It's also easy to note where schools and classrooms can fall down in their efforts to facilitate communication toward community.

Sometimes the work gets too hairy too quickly for those in positions of authority to be able to sit back and recognize that tumult is inherent in the formation of healthy group dynamics. Better described in the work of Bruce Tuckman,[30] groups develop in stages he's labeled *forming, storming, norming,* and *performing.*

Classroom- and school-level leaders see the first stage of forming happening at a relatively peaceful pace. Once a group enters the storming phase, though, many leaders mistake this for the train beginning to jump the rails. In actuality, this is a sign of the uphill trek of individuals figuring out who they are as members of the group. Finding new identities is never easy. If the difficult isn't seen as natural, many leaders will change course, thinking they've made a poor decision. Thus groups miss the chance of developing their own norms and, more important, of performing the tasks necessary to reach their common goals.

The classroom teacher who is willing to throw out a lesson plan for twenty minutes of students' finding their way to community hasn't left learning behind but has made space for a kind of learning often winnowed out of curricula in the pursuit of facts. The skills earned through the creation of community and navigating the experience of working with others are not only key to higher quality academic work but also the skills of advanced citizenship that schools should be fostering.

From Theory to Practice

- Find ways to create community that shares the responsibility of community among its members. Many teachers create classroom norms with their students on the first day of school; be willing to take the next step—create space and time for the members of the

classroom to revisit the norms, discuss successes
and failures, and revise the norms as needed.

- Create the space for the class (or the school) to develop
authentic projects that will have an effect on the community. Allow people to take real ownership, even if it means
that people will do things differently from the way you
would. If the only people in your classroom or your school
who can achieve leadership are those who would do things
exactly the way you would do them, the community will
never grow beyond your own ideas. If people—students
or teachers—can take your vision and make it their
own, the community will be one of true learning.

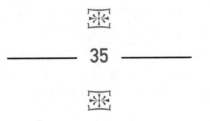

Say More, Talk Less

We talk a lot in classrooms. We talk a lot in schools. We talk
a lot in education.

Sit in any traditional classroom in America and you're likely
to hear much talking. Traditionally, this will be coming from the
teacher. Often it will be in lecture mode. If you (and the students)
are lucky, the class you are watching will feature a lecture from the

teacher and then time for the students to practice … alone … no talking.

If fortune turns his back on you, the lecture will last the entire class period, with the expectation that notes will be taken the whole way through.

In the schools we need, we say more and talk less.

Improvisational theater gives us an appropriate structure for considering this approach, it's called economy of dialogue. In her book, *"When I Say This … ," "Do You Mean That?"* Cherie Kerr explains, "What this means is the improv player can say only what is absolutely necessary during any scene in any show."[31]

An economic approach to talk in the classroom, well-deployed, can increase the value of what's being said. If a student no longer has to filter out the excess speech, it stands to reason those words he does hear will have greater value.

From a practical perspective, respecting the economy of dialogue also helps to adhere to Dan Meyer's directive, "Be less helpful."[32] With fewer words to instruct them, students will find themselves the chief technicians of their learning, needing to parse out the meaning of the judiciously offered information from the teacher.

This speaks to only one segment of the classroom population—the teacher—but the rule applies to students as well.

When we ask students, "Why?" after they've answered a question or offered an opinion, we are creating a semantic implication that there is a right answer for which we are looking. Sometimes there is. Much of the time, there is not. What we are after when we ask follow-up questions in class is more information from our students. We want them to say more to help us understand their thinking and help them to play out their nascent ideas.

If this is what we mean, then this is what we should say. In cases where students have offered information and our instincts tell us there is more to be mined in their minds, rather than narrowing the scope of what they might say next by asking "Why?" we can simply invite them to "Say more."

Let us as teachers practice economy of dialogue on our class-rooms, saying only as much as really needs to be said. Then let us ask students to say more so that they get comfortable with playing with ideas out loud and finding the meanings they intend to make.

From Theory to Practice

- Try changing from "Why?" or "What do you mean?" to "Say more … " in your classroom. Make a commitment to doing it for a full week and then journal about the experience at the end of the week. What did you notice that was different about what kids said in your classroom?
- Read *The Dialogic Curriculum* by Patricia Stock.[33] It is an amazing text for delving deeper into inquiry and into student ideas.

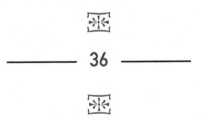

Be Deliberately Anti-Racist

In January 2014, Melinda Anderson wrote "How Long Will We Tolerate Racial Profiling in Our Schools?"[34] for *Good* maga-zine. It's an excellent piece that uses an experience her son had in school as a springboard for talking about zero-tolerance policies and the negative effect they have on all kids, and especially on children of color.

What was interesting and frustrating is that many commenters, both on Twitter and on the site, have pushed back that this incident had to be about race. "Zero tolerance," it is argued, "is bad for all kids, so why is this about race?" To make that argument is to ignore that zero-tolerance—and policies like it—have created an environment in which black students—primarily boys—are suspended at disproportionately high rates.[35] And the thing is, Anderson's piece pointed out that more progressive disciplinary policies, such as restorative justice (whereby students must work to restore whatever part of the community they have offended as a consequence of their actions), are good for all kids and good for kids of color.

There seems to be a difference between saying, "This is good for all kids, and it happens to be good for kids of color too … " and saying, "This is good for kids of color and good for all kids too." The first doesn't make inclusively humane practice the focus; rather, it places it as an afterthought. The second recognizes that we have to understand that school as an institution too often is authoritarian in nature, and those authoritarian practices, while bad for all kids, have disproportionately affected students whose existence is already on the margins of the dominant white culture in America.

Karen Mapp and Anne Henderson, in writing about ways schools can create better parent–school relationships, discuss the idea that parents bring the ghosts of their own experiences into their children's school with them.[36] We have to understand that our students do that as well. More than that, they bring all that they are—all their experiences—with them as well. For students who have reason to believe that the overarching society is not one that supports them, school cultures where punitive disciplinary policies are the norm can—and quite likely will—serve to further alienate them. We must actively work to ensure that does not happen.

As educators, therefore, we need to be cognizant of the work we have to do to create more equitable schools. It is of the utmost importance that we examine our policies, procedures, and structures to ensure that they do not reinforce the worst of what we see around us in the world. Restorative justice and other progressive disciplinary policies are powerful moments of "both/and." In pursuing both, we can make great strides to ensure that the work we do is good for students of color. What's pretty cool is that we'll create schools that are better for all children, too.

From Theory to Practice

- Say this out loud: "Schooling in America has long underserved children of color by not considering or understanding their needs. At our school, we will not continue this practice." When we name the problem, we stand a better chance of actually doing something about it.

- Choose a disciplinary policy in your school. Look at who is affected by the policy. If the policy disproportionately punishes children of color, change the policy. Ask what the underlying issues are, and work to create a culture change that finds ways to create a positive solution with fewer negative ramifications. Then, when creating new policies and procedures, go through the iterative process of asking how it will affect different populations, starting with historically underrepresented populations. Be intentional about creating systems and structures that are good for students who have be underserved and often made to feel that school was not for them.

- Recognize the time it will take. Changing people's minds and habits about anything is difficult. When race and ethnicity are in play, this is even more true. Know that it will take more than one training or difficult conversation to get your school where you want it to be. Know that the conversation will not end, and keep having it anyway.

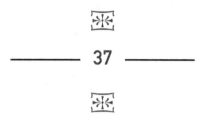

Practice Inclusive Language

While we can see the academic identities our students craft for themselves in our classrooms, we must remember their student-selves are not their whole selves any more than our teacher-, administrator-, counselor-selves are our whole selves.

There are other facets of our students' identities we must acknowledge even if we cannot know them as our own. One such facet, in terms of which schools have historically fallen down, is that of the sexual orientation of its students and their families.

The schools we need are spaces welcoming of students of all sexual identities.

Schools have come to accept (though arguably in a still painfully underexamined way) discussions of race, socioeconomic status, and learning differences, but not similar discussions of sexual orientation.

To illustrate the point, consider the last time you heard or participated in a conversation about race in a school. Perhaps it was in history class, maybe it was a discussion in an English course, or it could have been a variable studied in statistics.

In her book *Dude, You're a Fag*, C. J. Pascoe examines how schools work to reinforce heteronormative thinking and the othering of queer youth.[37]

Describing the implicit curriculum, Pascoe highlights the classroom of one teacher she studied, Ms. Macallister, as a "shrine to heterosexuality." Macallister's use of language was rooted in the assumption that all of her students could relate to examples of opposite-sex coupling and ignored relevant examples that might speak to LGBTQ students or their families.

Pascoe writes, "She instead reinforced, with the help of the students, a narrative of heterosexuality that depends on a similar age of the two partners, involves the state sanction of that relationship, and encourages procreation as central to such a relationship" (p. 32).

Ironic, too, is the fact that many educators would likely claim to be accepting of students of all sexual orientations, even taking on the moniker of "ally" to signify that their classrooms are safe spaces. The numbers, though, tell a story that perhaps the enacted beliefs in schools are not living up to those espoused by these open-minded teachers.

According to the 2011 Gay, Lesbian & Straight Education Network (GLSEN) School Climate Survey, "56.9% of students reported hearing homophobic remarks from their teachers or other school staff, and 56.9% of students reported hearing negative remarks about gender expression from teachers or other school staff."[38] While it's possible that none of these utterances was made by teachers who considered themselves allies of LGBTQ students, it's highly unlikely.

Creating a safe space for LGBTQ students means more than a sticker on the door and a showing of a selection of "It Gets Better" YouTube videos. It means thinking about the language we use in our classrooms, monitoring and discussing the language students use with one another, and considering the messages sent by the artifacts we use in our teaching.

Many teachers may point to the conservative views of local communities or discomfort or awkwardness with making explicit an effort to shift a normalized belief. The answer to these teachers must be, "Be the adult in the room."

We must remember that we are often the most powerful force for keeping our students safe in the classroom, and that each time we let hurtful or careless language or acts go by unexamined or unchallenged, we indicate tacit agreement. The message of that agreement does not serve our students, no matter their sexual orientation. It shouts that it is acceptable to "other" those in our community and suggests some people are worth respecting and others aren't because we do not care to understand who they are.

For those not ready to walk into the classroom and have a frank and open discussion of sexuality, the need for some time and reflection is understandable. The key, though, and the immediate step that must be taken if you are not ready to start tomorrow, is to stop doing and saying things that lead any students to feel as though they are less than. That, we can all do today.

From Theory to Practice

- Be deliberate in your language. When talking to students about relationships or families, do not always use heteronormative examples, especially when asking questions. Even something as simple as using non-gender-specific language when a student is talking about relationships can be powerful. We find that the word "someone" instead of a gendered pronoun can be powerful.

- Be public in your advocacy. Phrases like "That's so gay" or "No homo" are still heard in too many hallways in schools. Call student on their use of those phrases when you hear them. Have conversations about language with kids. Ask them what it means to use phrases like that and whether it makes for a safe environment for all students.

- Consider your content. Are you leaving certain groups and voices out of the content you ask students to study? When you do include LGBTQ people in class, are they limited to stories of coming out, depression, and hate crimes rather than stories of people living their lives as complete individuals?

- Connect to the work being done around issues of equity and education for students who identify as LGBTQ. Two places to turn are GLSEN (glsen.org) and The Trevor Project (thetrevorproject.org).

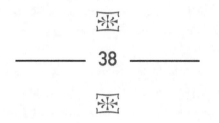

38

Honor Multiple Needs

Teachers' and students' interests don't always align. Sometimes it's for reasons that are easy to unpack—a teacher wants a student to do work that a student doesn't want to do for no other reason than that it isn't a subject of interest to them. Sometimes it's for much more complex reasons that involve issues of race, class, gender, and power that too often go unexamined in the halls and classrooms of schools. *This Is Not a Test* by Jose Vilson, *Other People's Children* by Lisa Delpit, and *I Won't Learn from You* by Herbert Kohl are three excellent texts about this—all are must-reads for educators, in our opinion.

This matters because we have seen, too often, different educational factions claim to speak for children in schools. This cuts across the edu-political spectrum, and we think it's time to stop doing it. No one has a monopoly on knowing what students need and want in any given situation, and it is almost a guarantee that if one tries to claim to be that voice, it is inauthentic. And yet, throughout the edu-political battles, you see organizations fighting over who best represents the children.

Let us simply say this: to state, "I know what is best for the children" is to run a deep risk of engaging in paternalism. And when that is coupled with teachers who are of different backgrounds—be they racial, socioeconomic, or anything else—there is an even deeper risk of engaging in colonial patterns of thought and behavior.

Our goal as teachers should be, simply, to help students to figure out for themselves what is best for them.

So we have to be honest about our institutional needs. We cannot and should not assume that students' needs are best served when teachers' needs are completely met. In fact, we can probably assume that they are not. And we would argue this: when we assume that teacher needs automatically and always trump student needs, we do damage. More to the point, we do damage to those students who are most likely to feel disenfranchised from societal institutions like school—often our students of color or our students from the most challenged economic situations. If we can reverse that trend, we will create policies in our schools that are actively better for students of color, with the added benefit of creating schools that are better for all students as well.

So how do we proceed?

This requires a deep shift in thinking for many teachers. It requires viewing the classroom as negotiated, cocreated space.

It also requires acknowledging that there is an inherent power dynamic between teachers and students that can make honest cocreation of space more difficult for students. It is, in fact, a risky proposition for a teenager to speak her needs—her truth—to a teacher who does not acknowledge the need to listen to it and take action.

There are ways to do this as a school community. Teachers and students can cocreate shared norms for the classroom. Students can be full voting members of teacher hiring committees. Project-based assignments can be open-ended to allow for student choice and voice in meaningful ways. But all of that can fall short of the goal of truly negotiated and cocreated spaces if there is not a mechanism for resolving the inevitable conflicts between a student and a teacher in a way that honors the needs of both.

Having an advisory structure in your school can serve one powerful purpose. The advisor–student relationship can—and should—include moments in which advisors serve as advocates and mediators when conflicts between students and teachers occur. The dynamic between a student and a teacher changes when another teacher is in the room with the express purpose of serving as the student advocate charged with navigating the space between.

By creating mediated spaces between students and teachers where student voice is valued and supported, we actually create the space for teachers and students to be more honest with each other. We have seen SLA teachers engage in some of the most profoundly vulnerable and honest moments with kids in these mediations. There is something very powerful when a teacher says to a student, "This is what I need." It turns out, it is a much more powerful moment than the artificial moment of a teacher trying to tell a student that something is actually good for the student when it's really what the teacher needs. It also creates the space for students to speak to their needs as well. And in the honest discussion of each other's needs and wants, we can find common ground. We can find compromise. We can find the space where we can come to agreement about the best solution for all parties, even if it is not the perfect solution for any one party.

In many ways, for many people, this requires a profound rethinking of the role of the teacher in the classroom. It requires more humility than many teachers are used to showing in the classroom, and it requires a great deal of inner strength to have that humility. It means understanding that although teachers are authoritative voices in the room, they should not be authoritarian. It requires understanding that there is an incredibly diverse range of needs in the room—including our own—and that navigating those needs is challenging. It requires learning more mediation skills than teachers are generally taught. It means inviting every other teacher in the building into your classroom as observer, advocate, mediator, negotiator. It means understanding that, while the outside world is very hard on teachers right now, that never—ever—makes it OK for teachers to lash out at others because of their own pain.

Finally, it means understanding that our classrooms and our schools will be better, healthier places when everyone in them can feel that in these places no one gets *everything* she wants, but each person can feel like she is heard, she is cared for, and she gets what she most needs.

From Theory to Practice

- Create spaces to listen to students. Whether this is an advisory program or simply monthly pizza lunch sessions where kids can feel safe to speak freely, schools need a feedback mechanism whereby the student voice is valued and valuable.

- Create committees that work on school issues collaboratively with students and teachers (and parents and administration).

Whether by ensuring that students are full voting members of a school leadership team or by giving real power to a Student Council, there has to be a place where the student's voice leads to active change; without one, students will quickly realize that their voice has no real power.

• Investigate how student voices are being heard in schools around the country. Students are using social media to talk about this. The organization Student Voice (http://stuvoice.org) hosts a weekly Twitter chat using the hashtag #StuVoice. Listen in. Take part.

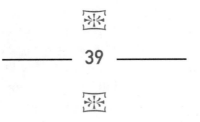

39

Listen to Understand

Faculty meetings can be fascinating.

Sit in the corner of a faculty meeting of any given school, just listen, and take a few notes. Based on what you see and hear, you'll be able to say much about what goes on in that school's classrooms.

Author Robert Fulghum,[39] writing about his time as a teacher, notes that he will go down in the history of his school as the guy who tried to kill himself with a pencil to get out of a faculty meeting. (To be sure, in no other setting is a pencil more likely to present itself as a weapon than in a faculty meeting.)

This needn't be so. One important skill to put into practice for transforming school culture among faculty is to practice *assuming positive intent*. When what you hear from those around you strikes you as hurtful, ignorant, or obstinate, assuming positive intent means pausing to make sure you're assuming the words you are hearing are meant to be helpful to the goals of teaching and learning in a caring way. This is not easy.

Another tool, equally as powerful and perhaps more important, is that of *listening to understand*.

In the schools we need, adults listen to one another to understand. They listen to the children with this goal as well. They listen to complaints about homework, assignment complexity, teaching styles, and the whole mess of issues. They do this with the assumed positive intent of the students, that they are working to get their needs met in the best ways they know how (and are not intending to anger the adults around them). If what we want for students we must want for teachers as well, then it makes sense to begin with the teachers.

Listening to understand is not a new concept by any means. For many, it is as simple as Atticus Finch's advice in *To Kill a Mockingbird*: "You never really understand a person until you consider things from his point of view—until you climb into his skin and walk around in it."[40]

It may seem like a long drawn-out process, trying to figure out all of the things that contribute to a person's thinking and then attempting to take on that perspective. If you were trying to do this for each member of a faculty, you'd likely retire before you'd completed the project.

Listening to understand actually means marshalling the forces of focus and curiosity to truly hear what another person is attempting to communicate. It means hearing not only what they are audibly saying but moving from those initial utterances to questions that show that you were listening and want to understand at a deeper level.

Here, too, community will be cocreated. Building understanding of those with whom we work helps us to understand how their goals, needs, and drives find common cause with our own goals, needs, and drives.

From Theory to Practice

- Look and listen. It's commonly known that the majority of communication is transmitted through nonverbal means. To truly listen to understand, you must listen with all of your senses. Pay attention to physical cues being sent your way.

- Ask. So often, our gut instinct in conversation when others are trying to explain themselves or make a point is to react with a statement of agreement or disagreement. If we take an extra beat, consider the information we have, and ask the next logical question, then the conversation and our understanding will be all the better for it.

- Say what you think you heard. In any line of communication, there is interference in the form of mishearing, getting distracted, or pouring our own thoughts into the process. By taking a moment to say to the person you're seeking to understand, "Here's what I think I just heard you say," we open the path for clarification.

- Listening to understand is different from listening to hear. While both are preferable to remaining quiet until it is your turn to talk, listening to understand has the benefit of developing purpose that is specific to those to whom we are listening.

——— 40 ———

✳

Learning Must Be Nonnegotiable

There's a trend we've noticed in education. Maybe you've noticed it too. Teachers are no longer teaching "students." They walk into their classrooms and find themselves teaching "learners." What's more, with this shift, many teachers find they aren't even teachers any more but have taken on the new title of "educators."

Many times it is easier to change what we call something and then point to it as innovation than it is to change what we do. We could insist that people start calling us male models tomorrow, but this would do little to attract the attention of agents, magazines, and the like if we didn't also change how we live our lives and what we deem important.

Such is the case with calling all people enrolled in a class learners. It's aspirational, and that's admirable, but changing what you call a thing means nothing if you don't also change what you are doing with regard to that thing.

Learning, on the other hand, must be nonnegotiable. It's a subtle difference, but a key one.

We don't care if our students are called learners, so long as our students are learning.

The latter is what's difficult to put our hands on. Perhaps this is why we've settled for the shift in name and decided to qualify the earning of that name with passing scores on exams of questionable worth.

The better answers come from teachers asking themselves, "Are my students learning?" and following that question with, "How can I tell?"

Building on that, the best schools and teachers are the ones that help students ask, "Am I learning?" and follow up that question with "What am I learning, and how can I use it?"

These questions prove to be difficult because of the possibility of negative answers. Either teacher or student is liable to answer "no" at any stage of the game. Such answers are invaluable, albeit frustrating. They represent the necessity of reevaluating what we've been doing, asking what isn't working, and then building something new with the knowledge we might need to go through this whole process time and again as we pursue learning.

The schools we need are not schools where students proudly introduce themselves as learners to those passing through, but schools where those passing through have no doubt that the work, play, and creation they see are acts of learning. They are also schools where teachers adjust their practice based on the learning (or lack thereof) they note in their spaces. It would be easy to look at a resistant or struggling student and, in words or actions, yell more loudly, "Learn better and more!" In fact, that is what many teachers do. If this works, it is by chance. If we are not getting students working at learning, then we must work to understand how each party is or is not working.

From Theory to Practice

- Use exit tickets in your classroom that ask students to be reflective about their own learning. Use questions such as "What did I do in class today?" followed by "What, if anything, did that help me learn?" Let them do so anonymously at first. Be willing to have conversations about trends you see in your classroom. Be willing to change your practice based on what the students tell you.

- Give students the chance to create artifacts of their learning. This is one of the keys of a project-based

classroom. What students create—be it a classic research
paper or a documentary video or a piece of original
computer code—should be a powerful showcase of
what they have learned. Consider asking students
to write a process paper in which they articulate the
"how" of what they learned, not just the what.

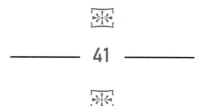

41

Ask Why the Kids Are in the Room

With almost everything we teach, we are always faced with
two very different challenges. One, what are we doing to
unlock the passion and skills of the 10 percent (or so) of the kids
who either already are or could become so passionate about our
subject that it becomes their course of study past their K–12 education? And two, what are we doing for the other 90 percent of
the kids? Why is it important that they are taking the class?

These goals often can feel at odds—from both a pedagogical
and a content perspective. But when we seek out goals that allow
all students to engage in active creation of relevant, empowering
meaning, we can honor the needs and interests of all of the students we teach.

When we look at the framework of backward-mapped unit planning tools such as *Understanding by Design*, we can teach from a foundation of enduring understandings and big ideas. We get to ask ourselves, "What will the students remember about this unit—about this class—twenty years from now? Which concepts and ideas are so important that everyone in the class has a reason to dive deep into them?"

This is our challenge—to help all the students we teach find the reason they are in our class. We must strive to ensure that the time we spend together will help every student become a better citizen and person, both today and in the future. Our classrooms must then be lenses on the world, not just for the students who fall in love with the same content we love, but for every child.

From Theory to Practice

- Read David Perkins' *Making Learning Whole*. Perkins writes about treating curriculum as teaching kids to "play the whole game." He argues that when we allow ourselves to stop seeing our subjects as atomized pieces of data to learn, we can see our students as learning junior varsity versions of the adult disciplines.

- Read *Understanding by Design* by Grant Wiggins and Jay McTigue. UbD is an excellent curriculum design tool that can help teachers think about why they are teaching what they are teaching, moving from teaching facts and figures in the order in which they come in the textbook to teaching big ideas and ensuring understandings. We believe that *Making Learning Whole* and *Understanding by Design*, used in concert, can provide an excellent conceptual and practical framework for curriculum design that is focused on the student.

———— 42 ————

Why Do We Need to Know This?

"Why do we need to know this?"

Many teachers hate and resent this question. Whether it is a reaction to the Shakespearean sonnet, the Pythagorean theorem, or the organization of the Periodic Table of Elements, kids spend a lot of time in schools wondering why they are learning what seems like a disconnected series of facts and skills that don't seem to have much importance to the lives they are leading. And from time to time, the bravest of students will screw up the courage to ask that question.

Sadly, too often the answers (when a teacher is even willing to engage with the question) range from "It is going to be on the test," to "It will help you some day," to "It'll help you get into college." When really, more often than not, it's because the subject matter in question is "part of the curriculum." If a student is lucky, the teacher is teaching that particular thing because the teacher has a real passion for the subject, but even that really doesn't answer the question in any meaningful way.

Students deserve an answer to the question. And we, as educators, need to understand that if we can't answer the question powerfully, we have to start questioning what we teach and how we teach it.

We live in a fascinating world. There's more really interesting stuff to learn, understand, and do than any one person has time for in a lifetime—or probably ten lifetimes. Helping students to see the power and beauty of all that stuff is one of the most important jobs of a teacher, if not *the* most important. That is where an inquiry-driven, project-based approach to learning is so essential. Specific questions like, "How do I be a better boyfriend/girlfriend?" "What pollutants are in the drinking water in my home?" and "How do we build—physically and philosophically—my ideal learning space?" can generate powerful answers to that perennial question, "Why do I need to know this?" All of these questions could have relevance to the students in our classes, and all of them open students up to the received wisdom of not just the teacher, but also the world at large. Equally as important, all of those questions could lead students to engage in powerful problem solving, artifact building, and reflection as they consider their personal answers to those questions.

If we remember that the time students spend in school is supposed to be about helping them to become better citizens, then the question "Why do we need to know this?" becomes essential to what and why we teach. The more specific questions and answers that follow the asking of the question should and will have profound implications on both our content and our pedagogy. And if we create our learning spaces as places where every student has the right to ask, "Why do I need to know this?"—where that is the first, most exciting question of every day—we can create vibrant, powerfully relevant classes that engage and empower everyone in them.

From Theory to Practice

- Sit down with an adult you respect in a field other than the one you teach. Go over the next few months of your curriculum (or the past few months) and see how much the other person knows. Does he know it? Does he have a passing memory of it? Does he use the information or skill in any way? If you give a final exam or if you have a state test in your subject, could he pass it? If the answer to any of these questions is "No" or "None," ask yourself what that means for what you teach and/or how you teach it.

- Ask what the students want to know. Maybe it will take a brief overview of the class and the intended curriculum, or maybe they'll come in with questions. Either way, ask students what they want to know about the content in which you specialize. Then—and this is key—work as hard as you can to shape their learning experiences around those questions. Often this will be at odds with the pacing guidelines of your district. So be it.

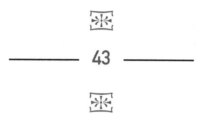

Deconstruct Passion

Ask most any teacher why she became a teacher and more likely than not, you're going to get a story of another teacher somewhere in the course of her academic career who brought her love of her chosen discipline to life.

You might hear the story of the English teacher who instilled a love of great literature and deep readings of texts through the classics. Another might tell you of a physics teacher who illuminated the wonder of understanding the world by seeking its most basic building blocks, or the math teacher who showed the artistry of balancing equations and solving for *x*.

Dig a bit more deeply, and these stories of "that one teacher" are likely to reveal hopes that these younger teachers can teach in the same fashion and shape for their students the same experiences that led them down their vocational path.

It makes sense that teachers would like to create the same sense of wonder she found in these classes for her own students, and this is not enough.

In the schools we need, teachers teach not as they were taught, but as students need to learn.

For each teacher who found his path through the practice of a single illuminating teacher, there were likely dozens of other students sitting alongside who were left in the dark. For whatever reason—and they were likely myriad—what happened in those classes didn't speak to many of the other students. While the English teacher was crafted into a lifelong reader and lover of words through a sharply focused examination of *The Great Gatsby* or *Pride and Prejudice*, she must remember in her own practice that she is responsible not for uncovering the handful of students who will also fall in love with these texts, but for opening up the world of letters to *all* her students. She is responsible not for convincing all her students to be English teachers or English majors, but for helping all her students find themselves in the pages of some text and being able to carefully consider what they find there.

This is difficult.

While we will often profess to want to help all of our students find pathways to learning, we generally create pathways that look much like those that led us to our own destinations. We find sanctity in trying to recreate the experiences that were created for us by our own teachers. Perhaps not explicitly, but certainly implicitly, doing what was done for us is a way to honor our past.

The better way of honoring that past in the classroom is by building a bigger tent. We must pause, deconstruct our learning experience—no matter the subject—and rebuild our classrooms and our teaching practices as hubs providing multitudes of entry points for any students willing to ask a question, voice an opinion, or challenge a long-held idea. It isn't enough, for example, to mirror the teacher who ran incredible class discussions in your favorite English class growing up, because as much as that may have inspired your love of reading, chances are there were students in that class who never found their voice. If that love of English is rooted in finding books in which you lost yourself, immersed in the world of the stories you read, don't recreate that reading list. Recreate that experience. Give students choice and challenges to find the books they love, not the books you think they should love. It's an important difference, and it means giving greater control to students—that is, control in the interest of passion. We can think of no better reason.

And yet, we must acknowledge that we stand on the shoulders of giants. We have learned from many before we ever stepped into our own classrooms, and we have, ideally, continued to learn as we have progressed in our careers. Without question, our classrooms should contain pieces of the best of the teachers who have influenced us.

Such classrooms take the best of the paths that led us from the teachers we learned from to the teachers we became, while recognizing that these are not the only paths to deep, passionate, and lifelong learning.

From Theory to Practice

- Make a list of five teachers who inspired you when you were a student. Ask yourself—what were the qualities that made them great teachers for you? Examine your own practice and ask yourself whether you see echoes of those teachers in your own teaching.

- Ask yourself—what kind of student were you? Is your teaching style unconsciously teaching toward the student you were? When you examine who influenced your teaching style in combination with the kind of student you were, can you identify the kinds of students who are left out of your natural teaching style? Are there teachers in your school who reach those students better? How do they do so? What can you learn from them?

⊞

──────── 44 ────────

⊞

Inquiring Minds Really Do Want to Know

Turns out, the two-year-olds have it right.

When they ask "Why?" it is a pretty important question. They are trying to make sense of their world, and although most parents can quickly tire of the question, those two-year-olds are on the right path. We want our students, years later in school, to still want to figure out their worlds; to keep asking "Why?"

So what happens in the intervening years? How do we go from the natural curiosity of the two-year-old to the practiced detachment of the typical teenager? What is it about school that teaches kids not to care about their work—and by extension, their world?

The ultimate stereotype of the American classroom is still to be found in *Ferris Bueller's Day Off*, in which Ben Stein is profoundly unable to get any student in the classroom to care about the Smoot-Hawley Tariff Act. And maybe the Smoot-Hawley Tariff Act is unredeemable; we don't know. But those kids in that class will never know because the teacher was asking questions he knew the answer to, and the students had one job—to parrot back those answers.

That pedagogical approach is long since past its prime—if it ever had a prime in the first place.

An inquiry-driven pedagogy is, at heart, about asking questions to which we do not know the answers. In *Zen and the Art of Motorcycle Maintenance*, Robert Pirsig writes: "A man conducting a gee-whiz science show with fifty thousand dollars' worth of Frankenstein equipment is not doing anything scientific if he knows beforehand what the results of his efforts are going to be. A motorcycle mechanic, on the other hand, who honks the horn to see if the battery works is informally conducting a true scientific experiment. He is testing a hypothesis by putting the question to nature."[41]

And while the overwhelming majority of teachers are very good at the "facts" of their discipline, we have to get better at using those facts to help students build meaning. We should be asking powerful questions that require students to apply knowledge, attack problems of their own design, and come up with their own "small *a*" answers.

Inquiry really requires people—students and teachers—to live in the uncomfortable places, and that's difficult. Inquiry requires that we all develop a nimbleness of mind so that we do not give in to the orthodoxy of our own ideas. That's important for students and teachers (and principals), so that we can start to really hone our skill of deep thinking.

And an inquiry-driven education does not preclude content—rather, it makes content all the more important.

For kids to tackle a problem they see in their community, they need to have a complex understanding of the problem before they can come up with a worthwhile solution. For kids to engage in deep inquiry and make real decisions about what they think and understand about complex issues, they must have synthesized a great deal of information.

To return to *Ferris Bueller*, it is the difference between simply having kids learn the facts and figures of the Smoot-Hawley Act and having students question the relationship between commerce and government, study the historical evolution of that relationship, and then decide for themselves what they believe should be the role of government in influencing the market.

And if we want our students to really be thoughtful scholars and citizens, don't we owe it to them to teach them how to think for themselves?

From Theory to Practice

- Use essential questions to shift your pedagogical approach from learning content to learning about why content has meaning. Wiggins and McTigue's book *Essential Questions: Opening Doors to Student Understanding*[42] is an excellent text for learning how to craft meaningful essential questions.

- Find needs, then help students find ways to work toward them. In one attempt to help students find legitimate nonfiction writing practice, Zac began by asking students for problems that they had identified in their individual neighborhoods. Each student came up with a list. Then they asked which problem they could most likely help solve and find the resources to solve. And then the real work began. Students started finding grants that could help them fund solutions to these community problems, did the hard work of writing grant applications, and submitted them.

Along the way, because the issues were myriad, Zac's main
role was in helping students to ask the right questions.
Because the issues were of import to the students, the
writing was tremendous, and the research diligent.

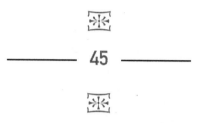

Ask What They Are Curious About

Sit in any classroom, traditional or not, and wait until the end.
Then answer this question: "What were the students in this
class curious about?"

It will be tempting, in this exercise, to answer with what they
were "supposed" to be curious about, what questions were asked as
a class via teacher redirection, or what you yourself were curious
about and thereby assigned to the students.

Don't do any of these things. Instead, look at the notes you
were copiously jotting down during your observation and try to
find direct, empirical evidence of student curiosity. If you cannot,
something is wrong.

This is one of our favorite questions to ask when debriefing a
lesson teachers have just taught. To do so reframes our reflection
on teaching in a way that looks to learning as a process of
exploration based on the naturally occurring questions and

wonder that come along with encountering new ideas. Ask any teacher more in love with their content area than anything else why they love that content, and they're likely to describe some formative experience when they started questioning and never quite found the motivation to stop. Sadly, these same teachers who are most enamored of their content often fail to hold enough back in their teaching to invite those same questions from their students.

Lessons in these classrooms often become, "I know this, and this, and this, and this ... and you should too." Students in such settings have no need for curiosity. The content is presented to them as if we have uncovered all the answers about that subject that are worth finding.

If our goal is to foster in our students the same sort of wonder that drives our own curiosity, we must realize the answer is *not* showing all that we know and can be known.

Instead, the answer comes from Kurt Vonnegut's eight basics of creative writing, as outlined in his short story collection *Bagombo Snuff Box*.[43] We don't even need all eight. One will do.

"Start as close to the end as possible."

To instill curiosity in our students (and ourselves), we must start as close to the end of the story as possible.

History classes serve as a fine example of this. In their most traditional sequence, these classes begin with the earliest recorded history and then move forward across the years. Oddly enough, since we began the teaching of history, more of it has taken place, but that might not be obvious in the contemporary history class. A student graduating from high school may have learned about the past through the end of World War II (maybe the Vietnam War, if she's lucky), but that is likely where history ended for this student because of our fascination with passing on our knowledge of how things are, starting with the earliest details as though they are inherently more important.

Imagine, instead, if we take a page from Vonnegut, and teach history starting as close to the end as it stands now and walk into a classroom saying, "Here's what happened in the world yesterday;

what questions does that raise?" Such a class is likely to face a time crunch, just as the traditional class did. But this time, that crunch will be students not having enough time to ask and search for answers to all the questions that arise, rather than the teacher not having enough time to lead an abstract field trip to ancient Mesopotamia.

If we ground our reflection in "What were they curious about?" and start our teaching as close to the end as possible so as to draw out that curiosity, we will have moved a long way to creating the schools we need.

From Theory to Practice

- Use exit tickets to find out what piqued student curiosity in your classes. Ask students questions like "Was there anything that made you want to know more today?" and "What follow-up questions do you have from today's lesson?" You can gather them in a Google Form/Google Spreadsheet and then publish and use the results to spur further inquiry.
- Have students keep question logs. These can be on paper, on their phones, on the board. Have students keep track of all their questions throughout a unit of study. Then free up time in your schedule—maybe a week or two—when you would normally prep for an exam. Instead, ask your students to find the meatiest, juiciest questions they logged during their study, and give them the time to find answers (and more questions). Allow the freedom of students choosing how they present their findings, and then give space in the classroom or in the larger world for students to showcase their new knowledge.

———— 46 ————

Understand What Project-Based Learning Really Means

Project-based learning is the easiest thing in the world to talk about because it's almost a guarantee that few teachers will disagree with you. Everyone will nod their head and say that it's a good thing. But true project-based learning is an inversion of our traditional classrooms in powerful ways. Here's why:

Project-based learning is not what you do after you've given the test, or as supplemental to the test, or as anything other than the primary method of assessment of student learning.

In true project-based learning you may give quizzes to check in or "dipstick" for comprehension, but when it comes time to assess what students really, deeply understand about a unit, they do an authentic, student-centered assessment—a project.

If authentic student work is not the highest-order assessment in a classroom, that classroom is not project-based. It is still relying on a teacher's sense of what students must know for its highest moment of learning. A project puts it into the kids' hands to demonstrate and apply knowledge, skills, content, and (if there's a reflective piece) metacognition.

Ask yourself, challenge yourself—if you really want to know what kids know and can do, how do you assess that? When do you really feel like you know what kids can do?

And ask yourself this: How much control do you give over to the kids every day to really own their learning? Have you ever been surprised by that moment when a student took a piece of schoolwork in a direction that was completely unexpected? And what did you do in that moment?

In the end, project-based learning isn't only about assessment. It is about asking what we can make and want to make, and how we will find the ways and tools to do that. It is about asking how our students' creations can show us what they have learned and need to know. Nearly everything in this book can be applied to this ideal. By labeling it "project-based learning," we both run the risk of reducing these ideas to less than what they are and also name it something that allows the greatest number of people access to the power these ideas can harness.

From Theory to Practice

- Examine your most recent unit of study. What assessment do you use to allow students to transfer the skills and knowledge of the unit to something of their own creation? Can you create an opportunity for students to tackle the big idea of the unit through an authentic artifact of their own creation?

- Remember the principles of situated motivation. When designing projects, it is tempting to lock the possibilities down. This makes projects look like tests. Instead, as you design projects, ask where you have left room for choice, challenge, collaboration, and control. At the end of a project, will you see student voice, or will you see students trying to speak with *your* voice?

——————— 47 ———————

We Need to Change the Way We Teach Math

It seems clear that we don't know how to teach math. We barely know why we teach it, or what to teach, either.

If we were teaching math the right way, it wouldn't be OK for so many people to feel comfortable saying, "Oh, I hate math." Yet you can be in a room full of really smart, successful people and all but guarantee that a substantial subset will say that they hate math. In the very least, they'll claim they aren't good at it.

That means we are not doing a good job somewhere. Somehow, in the "how," "why," and "what," we are falling down on the job. And because we don't do it well, math remains the third rail of progressive education. Our friend Gary Stager told us of MIT mathematician, computer scientist, and educator Seymour Papert's claim that math represents the failure of progressive education because the way we teach math always reintroduces coercion back into education.[44] To wit, even in most progressive schools, math is the thing we teach because "we have to learn it," and many progressive schools have struggled with the problem that their math classes have a distinctly different pedagogy than every other class in the school.

Yes, there are those who fall in love with the pure beauty of higher-level mathematics. For those of us who would have moments of epiphany when we could just "see" the math unfold in a way that seemed to explain the universe, math class could be amazing. But the fact that there are some folks like that seems to be used to justify not changing the fundamental pedagogy and structure of math, thereby ignoring all the kids who never understood or cared about a sine wave.

Conrad Wolfram's TED Talk[45] about the need to understand the difference between computation and real mathematics is a good start in helping to figure out how to do it better. Wolfram speaks powerfully about how true mathematics is not doing problem sets but engaging in logical problem solving. If we could move our schools toward that kind of mathematical thinking, we could transform how we think about math, both in our schools and in our society, and Wolfram's talk speaks to how technology could be used in service of that idea.

Instead, we seem to be using technology to move in the opposite direction. Many schools are now using tutorial software like Khan Academy to teach math. Some schools–like the iSchool in NYC—are trying to split the difference. They teach "the stuff" of math using computer software, and then try to use their project-based instructional time to have kids apply the math in their projects. Does it work? It probably beats sitting and listening to a math teacher write and explain the math on the board.

But it raises a fundamental question for us—why do we just teach math as opposed to teaching it as a part of other disciplines? Learning math through problem sets and the occasional poorly worded word problems seems just wrong to us when mathematical thinking is problem finding and problem solving of the highest order. Of all the subjects that have been damaged by siloing and a lack of true interdisciplinarity, math seems to suffer the most.

After all, math is the language of the physical world. There's more real math in the arc of a Frisbee in flight than in all the word problems in a textbook.

Math is also the language of probability. Any poker player who has to consider the odds to know if they are making a good bet is doing applied mathematics.

And let's not forget that the same mathematical problem-solving algorithms are involved in every computer programming challenge we could possibly undertake.

What if we completely rethought the way we taught math, so that everything was structured around using math to seek out and solve problems? What mathematical concepts would become paramount? What pedagogies would come to the forefront? And how many people could we finally get to say that they don't "hate math"?

From Theory to Practice

- Read Dan Meyer's blog, *dy/dan* (http://blog.mrmeyer.com). Start with his entry, "The Three Acts of a Mathematical Story" (http://blog.mrmeyer.com/?p=10285) and watch his presentation "Be Less Helpful" (http://vimeo.com/ 8129732). Dan's thinking on how to change the way we teach math within the structure of the math classes we already have is absolutely a must-read.

- Teach courses that require mathematical thinking. Schools can implement computer programming classes and engineering classes, preferably for math credit, not for elective credit. Offer statistics as a high-level math option for students, as statistics is a fantastic way to encourage and teach mathematical thinking.

- Stop thinking that math is the exclusive domain of the math teacher. More teachers can use math in their classes. History classes can use social statistics, science classes can do data analysis, and in all these courses, the language of math can mirror what is taught in math classes.

Instill a Love of Learning

The Common Core will finally tell us all that needs to be taught in school.

Really.

Stop laughing.

We mean it!

Perhaps it is time for us to admit something.

Beyond the old 3 Rs of reading, writing, and 'rithmetic—which, interestingly, are where Common Core has focused—we have no idea of the specific content every kid really needs to know by the time she graduates from high school.

At the high school level, most teachers end up teaching the subject they love the most, and the actual content ends up being some mix of what they are told to teach and what they most love within the subject. And of course, over the last decade, the content of the tested subjects have been defined by whatever is on the test.

And the arguments over what gets taught seem never-ending. When someone suggests something is unnecessary to be taught—or even unnecessary to be tested—it's almost guaranteed that someone will make the counter-argument for all the reasons why it is necessary.

We think we're going about that argument the wrong way.

The problem isn't that what we teach doesn't have power and relevance in real life. There are strong arguments to be made about why everything taught in a typical American high school curriculum is important for people to know. But we can see at least three problems with that argument:

1. As evidenced by the popularity of the TV show *Are You Smarter Than a 5th Grader?*, it seems clear that most people don't remember much of the content they learn in high school. (And high-stakes testing doesn't seem to be making that any better.)

2. There's a ton of content we aren't teaching in high school that is probably every bit as important as what we are teaching.

3. There is nowhere near enough time to teach all the content we could argue is important in high school—or in all of pre-K–12, really.

As English teachers, this became obvious to us when we realized that all the lists of "Books Everyone Must Read" that we came across were (a) woefully incomplete, (b) deeply subjective, and (c) more than we could ever cram into a four-year high school curriculum anyway. Worse, people keep writing really amazing books every year, but no one was making high school last any longer.

We came to realize that our goals for our classes were reasonably simple—we wanted students to realize that stories were lenses not only on other worlds, but on our own as well. We wanted students to learn how to take apart language and create meaning from text. We wanted students to develop their voice and their ability to make an argument, both verbally and in print. And we wanted kids to want to keep reading after they left our class.

For a long time, we thought that was the luck of being an English teacher—the skills we wanted to teach were applicable to so much good content (books) that it didn't matter what content we taught, really, as long as it was a good book—and we were both just arrogant enough to think that we knew what that meant. But the more we think about this idea, the more we realize just how much "good content" is out there. And much like the list of good books, that content keeps on growing.

More than anything else, we need to recognize that too often school fails at the one thing we should endeavor to do more than anything else—instilling a love of learning. Given all there is to know in the world, that probably is the most important thing we could do for our students, yet schools seem to do this really poorly for a great many students. That failure is ours, and it is one we must redress, no matter how hard that is.

Given all there is to know, it is even more important that we do take the time to make relevant and meaningful the skills and content we teach. The immediacy of the world we live in can feel (and perhaps is) more important in the moment to our students than much of the content we are trying to teach. Therefore, if we want to earn our students' attention, the onus is on us to always be willing to answer that question of "Why do I have to learn this?" with an answer that is more compelling than a grade on a test.

And we should always remain humbled before the vast enormity of human knowledge. When we, as teachers, are truly awed by all there is to learn, when we are humble about our own learning and knowledge, we may start from a better place with our students. We may be more willing to accept that the things they know are vital as well. And we may be more willing to find common ground upon which we can all build knowledge and wisdom.

The idea that we could cram all that we hope our students can learn and know into a "common core" set of skills would be laughable if it weren't for the fact that we're trying to do it.

In the end, the problem with the Common Core isn't that it is too broad, but that it is too narrow. It doesn't attempt to teach kids the most important thing there is to understand:

There is always more we can learn.

From Theory to Practice

- Sign up for something new. When we become content with our content, we run the risk of forgetting how to empathize with our students' learning experiences. Signing up for a course with skillshare.com, edx.org, or any one of a number of online offerings can be a way to turn on learning for you and turn your students on to learning. You needn't look only online. There are sure to be any number of courses available through local channels. The best course of action could be sitting in a colleague's classroom and committing to completing a unit of study alongside your school's students.

- Find ways to help students make their learning public. This doesn't mean everything needs to be published and downloadable online. It means asking students what they are proud of and want to share and then helping them to curate those collections of learning. If students have no work of which they are proud, take that as a sign that there's a learning blockage somewhere in the process.

49

Stop Deficit-Model Thinking

A few years ago, a vendor for one of the many online tutorial companies was giving a presentation at a principals' meeting. The vendor was talking about how students could work independently and teachers could get an instant report of all of their deficits.

Chris raised his hand.

"Does your software have a joy report?"

"Excuse me?"

"How about a passion report? Is there anything in your software that tells me what my students enjoy or are passionate about or are even really good at?"

The conversation didn't go well from there.

Whether we are talking about students or schools, too much of the conversation about education deals with fixing what is broken. We read article after article about all the weaknesses our students have, how low our rank is on the international tests, or which schools did not make adequate yearly progress (AYP). Or perhaps the most cruel of all, an article—about which teacher ranked lowest in Los Angeles—that may have led to a teacher's suicide.[46]

In reaction, at schools all over America, students are forced to "learn" in a way that befits deficit-model thinking. We make sure that students are doubled and tripled up in their worst subjects. Schools are reducing the amount of time students have music, gym, even science so they have more time to raise their test scores. It is as if the sole purpose of schooling for many kids is just to make sure that they are slightly less bad at the things they are worst at.

We have created a schooling environment where the sole purpose seems to be to ameliorate the worst of our students' abilities, rather than nurture the best of who they are. We have created an environment where "reforms" can label schools as failing without ever setting foot in them, solely on the basis of one metric.

This has to stop, not because we should accept the current educational landscapes as the best we can hope for, but because the "fix what is broken" model is getting in the way of the evolution we need.

If we want kids to care about their education, we are going to have to encourage their passions.

If we want kids to believe in themselves, we have to help them build on their strengths, not just mitigate their weaknesses.

If we want parents to believe that we see the best in their children, we have to remember to reach out, not just when something bad happens, but when something good happens too.

And if we are to ask students and teachers and communities to dream big about what they want the future of school to be, we have to ask them to take risks. We have to ask them to see beyond their current structures to envision the possible.

Deficit-model thinking will never get us there.

Yes, we need to make sure that we help kids mitigate their weaknesses. Yes, we need to make sure that schools are doing right by the kids they teach. But we must do that without creating an environment—in schools and about schools—that makes all of us in school think the worst of ourselves.

From Theory to Practice

- Commit to giving students feedback on their work that includes mentions of only what they did well and where they inspired you. Grading student work and providing feedback is a deficit-oriented task where teachers tend to be on the lookout for everything the students need to fix. Stop that, and commit to helping students see only what they do well. Without that, we are leaving it to chance or only assuming that students will see the worth of their work. That's a dangerous gamble when considered with the critique we freely provide.

- Give equity to all activities. If we think that math is important, let us think it is as important as Spanish, chorus, drama, and any other course that traditionally takes a backseat when we schedule "deficit" students into "math enrichment" or some other insultingly disguised course. Think of your least favorite food. If you were trying to get to appreciate that food, you wouldn't simply take two or three more helpings of it at every meal; you would combine it with foods that you enjoyed eating. You would find natural pairings for that food—and find joy in those pairings.

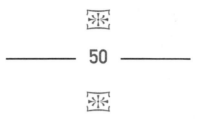

Start Surplus-Model Thinking

Students cross the thresholds of our schools as complete people, with lives, memories, and experiences embedded in their senses long before they begin first grade or fourth or twelfth.

We must not rest on the idea of students as neutral beings. Eliminating our assumption of difficulties is a start, but it is not enough. Agreeing that teaching is not designed solely to overcome deficits is only the first step, and it can leave us assuming students come ready for whatever we throw at them. Such a mind-set tempts us to throw whatever we like at these empty containers of knowledge.

Instead, the schools we need should operate on a surplus model of thinking about the students they serve.

For many, this shift will be a difficult. It will mean acknowledging that students come to us with more than we can imagine. It will mean a sense of humility that puts those who have been the kings and queens of their classrooms for decades in a difficult spot.

We must understand that the experiences students have outside of the classroom are more complex than whatever we could hope to set in front of them. They are certainly more complex than worksheets and packets of practice problems to be completed by the end of the week.

We must understand that the student who sets out before the sun rises and takes three buses to get to school has a greater understanding of systems thinking, motivations, academic preparedness, and internal locus of control than is likely to be taught in any civics or leadership class.

We must understand the complex narrative threads that exist in the communities of our students outstrip any put to page by Hemingway, Joyce, Dickinson, or Morrison. And we must up our game.

A surplus model of education means understanding the funds of knowledge that Luis Moll et al. found when they trained teachers in sociology, took them into students' homes, and asked them to keep track of the knowledge that was important and active in these spaces. As teacher researchers sat in homes and asked families about life at home, they began to recognize the complex funds of knowledge that students were bringing with them into classrooms. Managing a family schedule, caring for siblings, understanding family histories and traditions—these were all practical and applicable pieces of understanding that could easily help in meeting schooling goals.

A surplus model of education means looking at the work of the Institute for Democratic Education in America (IDEA)[47] and recognizing that they are tapped into educational organizations around the country who are doing right by the communities they serve. IDEA looks to, partners with, and celebrates community organizations that are doing good in neighborhoods and cities. The organization's focus is not on the deficits within communities, but on the successes and the ways organizations can network resources to build toward common goals.

This draws on another important surplus in education—teachers. We must recognize the wealth of knowledge our teachers bring to classrooms each day and free them to activate and implement that knowledge.

The teacher who can see that her students are coming to school hungry must be able to act on that knowledge and devise the creative solutions she knows will work by leveraging community partners to help her students access nutritious meals.

The teacher who knows that the district-prescribed reading curriculum is not truly helping his students become lifelong readers must be allowed to use his own knowledge to help his students find this love of letters.

The biology teacher who examines the scripted curriculum she's been prescribed and finds it wanting compared to the experiments, expeditions, and inquiry she has in mind must have the freedom to pursue and implement those approaches to make scientists of her students.

Our teachers and our students have a surplus of abilities and ideas simply by being human, curious, and present.

When we design systems that assume this surplus and operate on the belief that the people walking through our doors are capable and accomplished, what they will achieve will be awe-inspiring.

From Theory to Practice

- Have your students do a "strength assessment" at the start of the year. Ask students to tell you what they are good at—both in your discipline and outside of it. Ask them what excites them about school ... about the class you will share ... about learning. Read their answers often. Make decisions about your class with your students based on the class answers.

- Mention strengths aloud. Often, after any kind of assessment, teachers adjust course for the next unit of study and start focusing on where students fell short. Instead, after you've evaluated the learning, spend time in class sharing where individual students were strong: "Tyanne did a great job using specific examples in her writing. Talk to her if you'd like some help on that," or "Dennis's writing showed huge attention to details as he examined the texts. Talk to him if you're having trouble getting 'into' the book."

- Try out a variation of the 20-percent time in your class. Give kids the chance to work on projects of their own invention within the broad context of the course subject. Showcase what students create.

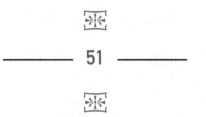

51

Assign Meaningful Projects

A aron transferred to SLA in his junior year after his large comprehensive school in Philadelphia closed. Toward the end of the first week, Zac asked him how SLA compared to his former school. It was similar, he said, with many of the same classes he'd seen where he came from.

"But that learning, though ... You guys are way ahead of us on learning."

It took time for him to become accustomed to the way of doing things at SLA. The transition was a culture shift, and it wasn't one he'd asked for.

If we had administered tests, we are sure we would have found gaps in Aaron's literacy and math scores. In conversations in class, he would often ask for clarification on historical ideas that were common knowledge to his classmates.

Using these pieces of assessment, we would have enough data to draw up a deficit model of Aaron that fit him somewhere in a remedial class in a traditional school.

That isn't the philosophy of the school.

If you want a dipstick along the way, use a quiz or test. If you want to know what a student has truly learned, assign a project.

Throughout his first quarter with us, Aaron was assigned a joint project through his English and history classes. He was to find a named building in his neighborhood and research both the building and the person for whom it was named. That done, he was to tell the story of both.

Aaron selected a middle school near his house and decided a video documentary would best convey what he found.

The physical structure of the school, Aaron found, had been under contract for sale to a local corporation. Though the contract had fallen through, the district had already installed a new heating system as part of the deal.

Aaron found that the heating system hadn't been connected or made operational, although the building was still being used as a school. It just sat in the basement unused while the inefficient system the building was built with limped along.

Then, Aaron found something else on the tour that changed the story he was telling. In the school's library, he found bare shelves and was told the school hadn't purchased a new book for the space in more than five years.

When he returned to SLA, he was impassioned. Recognizing the injustice he'd uncovered, Aaron approached the editing and production of his project with new intensity. He had found something real through the asking of authentic questions, and he worked to marshal all of his abilities to make the best product he could.

While Aaron's case is not the norm for all projects, it does highlight what can happen with projects at their best. Because he had been given the scope and charge to build something of meaning that required dexterity with primary sources, interviews, storytelling, and myriad other skills, Aaron created something that blew the possible deficit understanding of his learning out of the water.

Aaron's teachers were able to assess his discrete skills through quizzes and other assessments and offer Aaron help in augmenting the areas in which he was weakest. Because of the project, though, we were able to see the best of what Aaron was capable and, in turn, see the best of Aaron.

From Theory to Practice

- Give the full version. If the final assessment for the class just mentioned had been a test, many schools would likely have put a remedial version of that test in front of Aaron. Given the evidence, it would have seemed as though such an exam was all Aaron could handle. By assigning full, meaningful projects to all students, we remove the limitations our teacherly preconceptions can place on students and ask them to rise to the top of their thinking, rather than limiting them with what we perceive as their ceiling.

- Keep the options open. Attempts at projects should (a) include the ability to make what students want to make and (b) ask them to understand their decision-making process while they determine what they'll create. A twenty-slide presentation assumes that the knowledge and learning can fit only in that container, and that such presentations are the best evidence of every student's learning. This is never true. Ever. Giving students the option of how they present their learning will make the products richer every time.

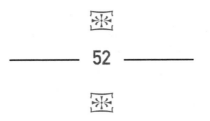

School Must Be Real Life

"You will need this some day."

All of us as teachers have said this to our kids at one time or another. As teacher tropes go, it is one that makes some sense to use. Why would a fifteen-year-old care about when the Magna Carta was signed? Why does a third grader really care about the different kinds of rocks?

But fifteen-year-olds do care about power dynamics and fairness. And third graders are fascinated by their surroundings. It turns out, understanding the world around you means understanding a great deal of the content that we teach. But it is up to the teachers to help the students make the connections between the world of school and the rest of their lives.

At EduCon 2.5, Philadelphia superintendent Dr. William Hite told the attendees that teachers must be masters of both content and context, imploring the educators present to make school relevant to the lives their students lead.

We would go one step further. It is not enough that we help students understand how important school is; school must help our students understand how important *they* are. David Perkins writes about helping students to play the "junior varsity" game of the world they live in.

At SLA, our students have built sustaining bio-walls; they have planned a major education conference; they have created public service campaigns; they have made original films; and they have interned at over one hundred sites all over Philadelphia. Whenever and wherever possible, we endeavor to help our students see their work as having real meaning now, not just that it might have meaning at some vague time in the future. Like the rest of our lives, not everything we do is the most meaningful thing ever done, but we strive to never teach in isolation, never give kids work that has no connection to the lives they lead.

This is at the heart of what we mean when we talk about inquiry-driven, project-based learning. And it is an important way we make sure that we work toward empowerment over simple engagement. Students will do the scut work necessary to make real connections and do meaningful work when students have ownership of the world and see how the work is important both to their lives and to the lives of others.

Adults rarely are willing to spend time learning things that are not of interest to them. All we have to do is walk into a school professional development session on the latest mandate from central office and see a group of teachers who look as disengaged as any stereotype of a teenager in a high school class could be. But walk into a school session where teachers are engaged in authentic action research or collaborating with peers on curriculum development, and you will see the learners we want to see in our own classrooms.

Why would we expect our students to be more willing to learn disconnected and inauthentic lessons than we are?

So it is incumbent upon us—in all classes—to find ways to make the work of the classroom have meaning. This means teaching mathematical problem solving so that students can apply a mathematical lens to the challenges around them. This means helping students to think like scientists and helping them do real scientific research and experimentation. This means teaching students that to think like social scientists and historians is to draw connections between the past and present, and that the space between the social scientist and the activist is slim indeed. And it means teaching students that the stories we read and the stories we tell have resonance in the way we learn, the way we live, and the way we work.

It isn't that we expect students to solve problems adults cannot. This isn't about overestimating the ability of children. It is about understanding that there are plenty of challenges that are hyperlocal or youth-oriented where they can make a difference either on their own or side-by-side with adults. And it is about understanding that we should not squander the energy and ideas of our young people by telling them that their ideas will matter beyond the classroom walls someday rather than daring them to share their ideas and make a difference today.

When we challenge students to make connections between the content of the classrooms and the context of their lives, school can be more than preparation for real life.

School can *be* real life.

From Theory to Practice

- Ask for problems. If you asked any organization in your community whether or not they would like pro bono access to thirty-plus consultants to help them reenvision a problem that organization was facing, you'd be hard-pressed to find an organization that would say no. So invite those problems into your classroom. Ask local non-profits, government offices, and community groups to enter your classroom and outline the problems they are facing. Then help your students structure building possibilities to solve those problems. There's no need for the teachers to manufacture problems. The world will take care of that.

- Have students become fixers in schools, and give them credit for it. Working toward a one-to-one technology-to-student program in your school? You probably don't have the budget you'd like for tech support for those devices. But we'd wager your students are curious how they might fix them. And those are skills that last. Have teachers who are anxious to build better lesson and unit plans to improve learning? Perhaps you could pair them with groups of students who have already completed a given course, then set up a unit review and suggestion group to offer authentic feed-back, from a student's perspective, on what might make learning click. There are more places to have students help us improve our schools than we often admit.

- Get outside the walls. Students at SLA engage in their Individualized Learning Plans[48] in tenth and eleventh grades, where they work with SLA's partnership coordinator, Jeremy Spry, to find placements at one of over one hundred partner organizations across the city. Students work in hospitals, schools, law firms, activist organizations, bike shops, college campuses, and every other organization you can imagine. Students have the opportunity to apply the skills they learn inside the school walls to outside organizations where they can see themselves as active agents in their world—in arenas of their own interest and passion.

53

Engage the Entrepreneurial Spirit

There is a lot of talk about making schools more entrepreneurial these days. People tend to immediately assume that means business, but we don't. Entrepreneurship is part of SLA's mission statement. But it's the part that often can be hardest to see if you don't know what you're looking for. We don't have lots of business classes, and a great many SLA graduates have expressed more interest in prosocial careers than in traditional business careers or even start-up careers.

But entrepreneurship is about so much more than a career in business today. The social entrepreneurship movement has shown us that the non-profit, prosocial world can be entrepreneurial as well. So what does it mean for a school to engage the entrepreneurial spirit?

In the end, what we believe is this: The entrepreneurial spirit is about owning your ideas and doing interesting, powerful things with them.

And we don't mean "owning" in some sort of proprietary nonsharing sort of way, because collaboration is a huge piece of entrepreneurship. It is about owning your ideas in the sense that you know your ideas have power and have meaning and have use. Ken Robinson defines creativity as "having original ideas of value."[49] That's not a bad place to start. Entrepreneurship is doing something with those ideas.

We think that school, as it is currently configured in most places, does not allow students or teachers to do that well.

That has to change. An entrepreneurial school is one where everyone—students, teachers, and administrators—understands that they can own their ideas and create powerful, useful artifacts of value. And we believe an artifact doesn't have to be static. Whether by a student writing code that will be incorporated into a function of the school's website, or a teacher creating and sharing empowering unit plans, or community members coming to school to build programs that enhance the lives of those in the community, schools must be entrepreneurial.

The challenges our students will face as they venture beyond our walls and deal with an ever-changing world will require the entrepreneurial spirit no matter the sector of society in which they live and work. The challenges our teachers face as they look to change schools from the 1950s model to the modern model will require passion, creativity, and the drive to see ideas through. The challenges we all face as our world changes at an ever-quickening pace require a flexibility of spirit, a collaborative sense of purpose, and the nimbleness to adapt to rapid change.

There are few institutions in our society that are currently configured to handle this change. Schools, by virtue of the very fact that they teach the young—those who will have to see this change through—must take the lead in revaluing and redefining the entrepreneurial spirit. Students must leave our walls with the confidence and skill to bring new ideas to bear on a society that desperately needs them.

From Theory to Practice

- Encourage ideas, and lower the threshold for implementing them. At SLA, if a student wants to start a new extracurricular group, she need only propose it and find a faculty member to sponsor the group. Sometimes, when no faculty member can be found, students connect with outside experts and bring them into the school to help. These relationships have forged some of the tightest bonds the school has with the larger Philadelphia community. As a small group of adults, we don't have the time or capacity to create and keep up all the connections the school currently has. As a community of learners that includes adults and children, our capacity is greatly increased.

- Include students in decision making. Whenever a new member joins the SLA community, student and teacher voices count in equal measure. Each of our interview committees includes students who sit alongside parents, administrators, and teachers and then help to select the appropriate new faculty members for the staff. These aren't the same students time and again. Sometimes they are asked as students of the classes to be taught, sometimes they are catch as catch can. All students stand an equal chance of having the agency and voice to make these decisions and contemplate what and whom it will take to sustain the community.

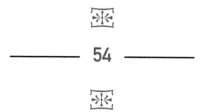

—— 54 ——

Classes Should Be Lenses, Not Silos

In our current incarnation of school, classes are essentially silos of information that are specific not only to a discipline, but also to a subset of information in that discipline. Not just science, but biology. Not just mathematics, but geometry. And so on. That creates a rigidity of thought in both student and teacher.

And while there is a lot of talk about interdisciplinarity these days, too often that just means that science teachers use some math in a project or an English class reads a Civil War novel while the U.S. history teaches about the Reconstruction. But that misses the power and potential of what is possible when we see the intersections of our courses as more than just the occasional overlapping project.

As long as we continue to be bound by the regulations of teaching specific courses, we should strive for the idea of viewing our courses as lenses, not silos. In this model, we learn science so that we can apply a scientific lens to the world around us. History becomes about exploring a case study and using the tools of the historian to learn from a moment in time and determine what lessons it holds for us now.

And those tools can transcend the courses when students go on to ask real questions and solve real problems. This is what leads SLA students to analyze pollution trend data in a science class, overlaying socioeconomic data with pollution data on the map of Philadelphia and asking questions about what they find; or take on a local issue of importance to them in an English classroom and design and implement a direct action campaign to affect change. Or when they do real-world data modeling in an Algebra I class, using variable manipulation to solve architecture problems and make sports forecasts. Or write essays on identity in Spanish while designing masks that are representations of who they are.

And these projects are not specifically "interdisciplinary" in that they don't have to be joint projects between two teachers. They are an ancillary benefit of teachers seeing themselves as teachers of kids before being teachers of subjects. It gives the students' use, application, and transferal of the skills and information a much higher priority than merely learning them. And you know it's working when teachers no longer have to be the drivers of interdisciplinarity; rather, it's the students themselves drawing the connections between what they learn in different classes and bringing their ideas to bear on the problems they want and need to solve.

From Theory to Practice

- Stream students in courses, so that students take a group of courses as a cohort. At SLA, students take English, History, and Science as a cohort in ninth through eleventh grades. Students and teachers work in the same groups all year, thus increasing the likelihood that ideas will resonate across classes.

- Use grade-wide themes and essential questions as throughlines for students to come back to that are not specific to one discipline over another. At SLA, the ninth grade theme is Identity, the tenth grade theme is Systems, and the eleventh grade theme is Change.

- Talk to your peers about how they're examining topics and themes in other disciplines, and use that knowledge to shape how you introduce ideas in your class. Students should not be surprised when their English teacher asks, "I know you're thinking about the question of identity at the genetic level in biochemistry. How does your understanding of that word shift as you begin to write your literary autobiographies?"

——— 55 ———

⌗

Create Complexity, Not Complications

Hugh MacLeod's cartoon, "Strive for Complex, Not for Complicated,"[50] is a powerfully crystallizing lens for thinking about the need for common structures, common language, and common processes in schools.

One of the great things about inquiry-driven, project-based learning is that it lends itself to incredible complexity. Whether it is creating a full-sized catapult or a documentary film or a biowall or any number of equally complex projects, truly inquiry-driven, project-based learning asks students to take their own ideas, marry them to the skills and content of a class, collaborate with colleagues, and create profound artifacts of their own learning.

The good news is that this kind of work is inspiring, challenging, and profound. The problem is that complex work is difficult. It requires kids to problem solve, to collaborate, to bring multiple skills to bear on solving a problem. As such, we have to make sure that the structure of school does not create complications that get in the way of complexity.

This is why it is so important for schools with a focus on the complex work of inquiry to set up common school structures so students can avoid as many complications as possible. To do this, the adults need to ensure that words mean the same thing from classroom to classroom; that goals build on one another, year to year; and that there is a common language of assessment so that students have a transparent sense of what is valued.

> At SLA, the work we have done on building a deep understanding of the way we use our core values and the way we use *Understanding by Design*—creating a common language of assessment with our school-wide rubric and our standards-based grading—has all been in service of creating a common language of learning. We want to lower the bar of understanding what the adults are asking so that we can raise the bar for understanding how to do the work—and understanding ourselves. The idea that we can come together around a vision of education and then do the complex work of creating a pathway to enabling that vision means that we can cut down on the amount of time kids get lost in the space between the adults. That has been one of the keys to our success. And it is a never-ending process of deepening our understanding of our processes and evolving our language to become more and more transparent to students. That commitment allows us to continue to grow together as educators and therefore help our students grow as well.

Anything we do in our schools and our classrooms that makes a student's life more complicated is time we steal from them to learn how to deal with the complexity of the problems they can tackle. As teachers, we need to examine our own practices to ensure that we do not get in the way of the powerful learning of our students.

From Theory to Practice

- Decide what you value, and speak to it in all you do. SLA had the advantage of building a school from an idea. Many people reading these words will be attempting to transform an existing system. The same kind of demystifying of common language is still possible. Ask your faculty and your students to list the words and phrases they hear most often in relation to teaching and learning. Document those utterances, and have all faculty document them. What do you notice that you can agree is working against success? Stop saying those things. What do you see that is aligned with the work you're trying to do? Agree to use those as often as possible. What's missing? Come up with the terms and ideas you agree as a faculty are important enough to adopt school-wide. This will be a continuous process requiring constant curation. Commit to returning to these ideas whenever possible.

- Avoid "excellence." This and other similar words have broad amorphous meanings that sound good, but can't be nailed down. Each of our core values at SLA works as an idea and a practice because teachers and students understand them as concepts to be observed. We can see when reflection is happening and tell people about it, because it is obvious.

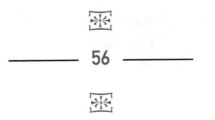

Find Something Interesting and Ask Questions

On the pavement of a running and biking path are two images left by an anonymous stencil artist. The first is a profile of a woman wearing a hijab. Slightly lower and to the

right of this image is another stenciled image of what could easily
be a mid-twentieth-century pinup girl.

Below the woman in the hijab is a single word "Oppression?"
and below the pinup girl, "Liberation?"

While some might see these images and bemoan the deface-
ment of public property, there is much more to be found in this
small stretch of sidewalk.

There is a quarter's worth of deep curriculum here that could
push the most precocious students to challenge their beliefs about
the world.

What is public property?
What does it mean to be liberated?
What does it mean to be oppressed?
How is gender defined across cultures?
How does your view of the world influence your understanding
    of how other people live?
What does art do?
What should art do?
Who decides the value of art?
When might it be acceptable to break the law?

The questions are potentially never-ending. They should be.
Good, thoughtful teaching and learning is a process more generative of questions than of hard-and-fast answers.

In the schools we need, the world provides a curriculum rife
with opportunities for questions, and the people within these
schools recognize these opportunities for what they are and
could be.

The images on the sidewalk need not come packaged in an
aligned, approved, and adopted curriculum. They need only come
from an individual who has developed the habit of mind that
allows, "Hmmm, that looks interesting," to be followed by, "I'll
take a picture of that and see what we can do with it."

In the simplest of terms, this process starts with classroom
teachers. At least at first, this is likely the only way to cultivate

such curiosity (especially given the neglect of educational curiosity that many children face in schools). Given time, though, this will become the culture of the classroom. Given more time, it will become the culture of the school.

Most important, given space, this will develop an understanding that neither classroom nor school is defined by the walls of a building or the designations outlined by a district.

For any of the questions just listed, the only material necessary for diving down the rabbit hole of inquiry is a device to capture and share the image to be examined. If the questions are being asked in a school with Wi-Fi access and a "bring your own device" policy, excellent. If it is a school with access to one-to-one computers, superb. A computer cart or lab? Tremendous. A library within the school or down the street? That'll do nicely.

In the same way that schools must learn to follow questions and allow them to generate more questions, they must consider resources as being generative as well. After "What are our questions?" teachers and students next must ask, "How will we find answers?"

Some spaces with overly abundant resources and close community ties will find the process easier to navigate. Those schools with limited access will find it more difficult. But in our experience, no matter how difficult the process, you can always rely on a set of communally generated, worthy questions.

If students need to find answers, they will find them. This will not change the difficulty of the process in the most isolated schools of Appalachia or the poorest of urban schools. It will, however, make that difficulty surmountable.

A camera and the openness for questions. From there, it's hard to imagine anything standing in the way of learning.

From Theory to Practice

- Start in faculty meetings. Ask teachers to capture images they find inspiring and educational in the time between meetings. While faculty are congregating at the start of the meeting, project the image. To start things off, ask what people think of the image, what questions it raises, and how they could incorporate it into their own practice. Creating these spaces in faculty meetings gives permission for teachers to create them in their classrooms. Mandating a practice won't do it.

• Make it standard practice for students to capture any images that catch their attention. Whenever it feels appropriate, ask students to send you the images they capture. Use these images to spark conversation. Sometimes they may be aligned with a specific curricular focus. Sometimes they won't be. Either way, it will encourage students to see the learning possible in the world around them, and it will invite them to share their curiosity with others.

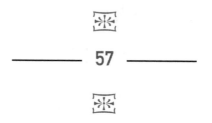

Story Matters

Each spring, a group of SLA juniors leaves the familiar confines of Philadelphia for the foreignness of Flagstaff, Arizona. They go as part of an independent trip in which they and ten students from Flagstaff raft down the San Juan River for four days, experiencing nature and the American landscape in a way few people ever have the chance to do. Along the way, they stop, disembark their rafts, and study collections of ancient petroglyphs left by Native Americans in a time long forgotten.

While archeologists have theories as to the meanings of these alien pictures, we don't quite know for sure. Each year, students stand near the walls and wonder at the remnants of a people and what they have left behind.

Story matters.

This is most obvious in English and language arts classrooms. Built on narratives, both fiction and nonfiction, their purpose is to connect story to its parts while helping students access both the whole and the pieces so that they may interpret the world. Story most clearly and forthrightly matters in these classrooms.

Where we fall down in appreciating story, but where it is no less necessary, is in the classrooms not traditionally thought of as the homes of stories. Math, Science, even History classrooms are often thought to be devoid of story or of the requirement of story.

Here is where stories are most necessary.

They need not be the stories of content. While helpful, it is not required that students know the stories of Pythagoras or Euclid. If they learn them, fine, but they are not required.

What should be required, and what should weigh on the minds of all teachers, are the stories each of their students lived before they became part of this class in this school. What were their math, history, science, English, physical education stories before they walked into our classrooms?

Almost inevitably, we fail to ask for our students' stories of prior experiences in school with specific regard to whatever subject matter we're charged with transmitting. When those stories are exchanged, when a student finds an unlikely mechanism for alerting her teacher to the story of how she came to think of herself as always deficient in math, we have few mechanisms for honoring those stories.

Instead, we charge through, foolhardily focused on curriculum timelines and learning objectives without concerning ourselves with what should be our own learning objectives—understanding where our students are coming from and how we might tailor our practice to meet them. Our goal should be to relate our lessons to their stories so that our chapters in their stories might be more fulfilling.

This is difficult work. It requires asking questions whose answers we may not like. When we were English teachers, each year we heard new students exclaim that they did not like reading, abhorred writing, and didn't even want to look at whatever it was we might consider "classics."

The instinctual response was not surprising. We put more classics in front of students, assigned reading quizzes. Asked comprehension questions. Talked of why others had loved these books. We did this over and over again. If we could only flood students' minds with enough great literature, we reasoned, surely their defenses would fall.

They didn't. Those students who read did so under great duress. Those who didn't created mechanisms for faking the reading or became greater distractions in class.

Then we changed our approach. Before forcing others' stories on them, we asked students to write their own stories. "What is your biography as a reader?" we asked. We sought to find out what had happened to them in each English class before ours. Were they spaces of exploration or narrative punishment? From there, we could see the educational scars they carried, and we realized that we needed to take a new tack. Choice must be paramount.

It is understandable for the classroom teacher to assume that the blank slate of the school year applies to whatever subject area she is responsible for. But this is not so and can never be so.

Given this, we must listen to the stories our students bring with them to our classes. We must listen to them as the first and most important pieces of data available to us in crafting learning experiences that might lead to better stories for our students.

From Theory to Practice

- Whatever your subject area, ask your students for their educational biography before they entered your class. Did they enjoy the content area? When did they fail? Why? When did they succeed? Why? This doesn't need to be a written report. It need only be a chance for students to share a narrative of the classes that have come before yours.

- Evolve your own teaching to help them write a better story. Use this data that students have provided and look for trends and opportunities. If a practice or approach to content didn't work for the majority of students, avoid it. If they are scared, find a way to alleviate those fears. If they have expertise, draw that out. Give their narrative data the same weight that you would give to a test score or attendance data—or even more.

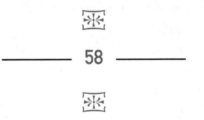

—— 58 ——

Success Is the Best Weapon

Zac had an idea at the start of his first year of teaching. A friend had given him a book as a graduation present. It was full of useful tips and instructions for life, and he thought it could provide a helpful jumping-off point for conversations about citizenship and what it meant to be responsible members of society.

Zac was teaching eighth grade at the time as part of a middle school team model. He shared all of his students with the same social studies, science, and math teachers. The team leader was our special education resource teacher.

Incredibly aware of his novice status and not wanting to be a young upstart, Zac kept to himself his hopes that the entire team might adopt the book and create a united front.

Instead, he decided to quietly begin implementing a piece of the book each day. It took from five to ten minutes of each class and incited some thoughtful conversations about what might be the best ways to be a person who is part of a whole.

Although in hindsight he would probably teach the individual lessons differently—and would probably choose a different book—the tack Zac took was the perfect one.

After a month of daily citizenship discussion, two of the other teachers on his team asked about the book Zac was using and if he'd give them a heads up on the topics they'd be discussing each day so they could reinforce it in their classrooms. They'd noticed students interacting differently in their classrooms—acting more civil—and they wanted to be a part of it.

Zac gladly obliged. By the end of the first quarter of the school year, all the teachers on the team had adopted the book in their classrooms, and it had become the common language of their team.

Though Zac had given up the idea of changing team culture as a first-year teacher, that was what he'd ended up doing.

Success was the best weapon.

Another time, a fellow teacher asked about project-based learning. She worked with a conservative principal who enjoyed textbooks, quizzes, and tests. He was a good guy, the teacher said, but she had no idea how to warm him up to the idea of project-based learning in their school.

The answer was simple: "Do it in your classroom. Do it well. Share your successes." If she could show her principal that his goals were achievable through the means she was advocating, he'd be much more likely to at least consider a more widespread application of those means.

Until he could see actual success, the theoretical was much more frightening and uncertain than whatever approach teachers in their school were already using.

For most people, change is loss. Until they can see that change (and loss) as a sign of increased success, people will shy away from the prospect of the new.

If Zac had stepped into his first team meeting of the year, unproven in the classroom, and suggested to his teammates that they all adopt the same book and share the same conversations with students throughout the year, he might have raised some curiosity, but it's doubtful the team ever would have achieved the same shared ownership by the end of that first quarter.

By implementing an idea on a small scale where you can nurture it and improve it along the way, you will be able to cultivate success.

As success grew in Zac's class, it became attractive to others. It wasn't an idea from a teacher with no experience. It was an idea drawing kids into learning and reflection.

Success was attractive, and it proved the best weapon for change.

From Theory to Practice

- Start small and set reasonable goals. This can be frustrating—and it certainly isn't what we did at SLA—but it also can be an incredibly effective strategy when an entire organization isn't pulling in the direction you want to go. Big, hairy, audacious ideas are awesome— we're big fans of them—but not everyone can take a leap of faith without seeing what it looks like with their own eyes.

- Share credit. Ideas don't grow when they are held too close to the vest. If you got permission to try something risky, the person who gave you permission was an important part of your success. If a colleague was there to bounce ideas off of, that person is part of your success. We all want to be part of something good, and when that good thing is shared, we can build from there.

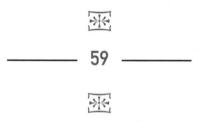

59

Preschool Is a Great Model

One of our favorite school-related spaces is any preschool classroom. Everything is colorful, snacks are provided, and nap time is a regular occurrence. It strikes us sharply how in tune preschool teachers are to the needs and development of their students. They build a constant state of play and exploration while providing boundaries to keep students from activities that might be less than safe.

As if this weren't enough, these teachers are also constantly talking about caring, with questions like, "How do we treat our friends?" "Why do we share?" and "How can we make Isabelle feel better?"

Blended with colors, shapes, and their first experiences with reading, preschool students are wrapped in a curriculum of care that serves them well as their worlds expand beyond their homes and beyond their classrooms.

The further up the school pipeline students progress, the further they drift from this complete curriculum.

By the time a student hits high school, when his frontal lobe could best be described as a lump of protean goo, long gone are questions of how friends should be treated, the benefits of sharing, and the best ways to help others feel cared for. For no good reason, we attend to students' needs as people less and less as their personhoods become more and more complex.

We do this with few, if any, other parts of school. In academics, school systems all over the country are working on ways to track student performance for the first sign of trouble, but we do little to check in on the social and emotional health of our students.

Chances are, at most schools in America, a student can count on one hand the number of times he can screw up in his math class before the switch is flipped to some sort of remediation, teacher meeting, parent call, extra classes, and so on. Schools will marshal an armada of resources at the first sign of trouble in core academic subjects.

A sad student, though—one who is consistently withdrawn and unhappy—can go unnoticed, unsupported, and uncared for throughout all of his high school years (if he makes it through high school). Schools do a amazing job of operating as though this sadness couldn't be linked to the math madness just described and, whether it is or not, it doesn't have to be their business.

A school designed to meet the needs of all people within its walls would function consistently with the mind-set of the preschool teacher and would completely understand the need to continue supporting students' inquiry into what it means to be a contributing member of a community and a thoughtful friend.

The adults in these schools will feel a compulsion to, as much as possible, see their students as full people and not as sponges, vessels, mounds of clay, or any of the other clichés frequently used to describe them.

Learning to shift their perspective could be something as simple as following author and educator Hal Urban's[51] suggestion to begin class by asking students to share what good news they have to report about their lives.

It could mean sending a note home to the adults in a student's life, letting them know that you noted how much work he put into moving his grade in precalculus from a D to a C. In its most basic form, it means working with students when they've made poor choices, and helping them to reflect in a way that doesn't come naturally for either the preschool or adolescent brain.

A preschool classroom is a happy place. Would that we were able to say the same about all classrooms.

From Theory to Practice

- Make your classroom space a physically joyful place to be. Whether that means finding a few beanbag chairs to create a reading nook in your classroom or having students design the walls with their own creations, make your classroom a cocreated space where people want to be.

- Share the awesome. When people do wonderful things, say so. Send happy emails home to parents. Take more joy in student accomplishments than you show sadness when students fall short of expectations. And end every class with a quick recap of good things you saw in class that day.

—————— 60 ——————

Every Kid Needs a Mentor

In a conversation about changes in social expectations of children in communities, juvenile advocate and community organizer Jolon McNeil remembered her own childhood in comparison with the worlds and schools of the children she dedicates her life to helping. "If I had gotten suspended," McNeil said, "everyone in my family, everyone in my community, and everyone in my church would have kicked my butt."[52]

It's different for today's students, McNeil says. Because of a disconnect between schools and communities, for many the level of home awareness and community consequences that she knew has faded into the past.

While few would argue that school should or could step in and take the space of the family, community, and faith organization, there is something that schools can do that requires minimal resources and improves the lives of everyone involved.

Every kid needs a mentor.

Mentoring builds social and cultural capital in students, connects them with singular adults whose purpose is to support the student, and connects them to an anchor in the community.

For the community, the benefits are equally plentiful. Mentoring is an investment in the community—not an economic investment (though that argument can also be made), but an investment in growing the kind of citizens, neighbors, and community leaders whom mentors want to live alongside in the coming years.

To be certain, teachers can be and are mentors to the students they teach. We spend more time with our students than many of them spend with their parents in the later grades. Connecting with students on online platforms like Facebook is a form of mentorship in that we can model appropriate behavior, find connection with students who are feeling lost and can't bring themselves to make contact face-to-face, and step in as adults when students push too far past what is acceptable conduct in any community—online or off.

Expecting teachers to be full mentors is placing an insupportable weight on their shoulders. The deep connections inherent in a full mentoring relationship require time and personal commitment impossible with a roster of 150 students.

However, schools can be the conduits and catalysts for mentoring relationships. Here's an example.

Wanting to match as many of its students with mentors as possible, Phoenix Academy, a magnet high school in Sarasota, Florida, that recruited only the lowest-achieving students in the district, sought to build its capacity to meet its goal by partnering with those already doing the work.

The school contacted the local Big Brothers Big Sisters (BBBS) office and explained their goals. BBBS said they could help. In a matter of weeks, the school welcomed representatives from the organization into the school one evening. Also in attendance were those community members school personnel were able to recruit into mentorship. Throughout the course of the evening, the would-be mentors navigated the school district's volunteer clearance procedure and received BBBS orientation training and clearance checks en masse.

By the night's end, Phoenix Academy had scores of new mentors on call to match with its students, and BBBS had made contact with many community members with whom it otherwise would not likely have connected.

Most important, in the weeks that followed, Phoenix students were matched with caring adults from the community in whom they could find a friend, advocate, and mentor.

These kinds of partnerships are possible in communities and schools across the country. They need only a school willing to set the goal and make the initial investment in organizing the effort.

We know the benefits of mentoring and community connections and the strength of shared vision and goals.

We need to match kids with mentors.

From Theory to Practice

- Build a mentor database. Find people in your community willing to spend some time with the students in your school. If you have a local chapter of BBBS, use them. If you don't, reach out to other local organizations that have volunteer programs. Find reasons to bring mentors and students together physically at school when possible. Chris's son's public elementary school brings in retirees to read with young students. SLA pairs seniors with mentors from outside school for their Capstone projects. There are many ways to do this.

- Leverage alumni. This is something we are planning to do at SLA as soon as we have enough graduating classes to make this sustainable. Imagine that the first time a student logs into her school email address she finds an email from an alumnus of the school letting her know that she will always be able to reach out for help. Wouldn't that be a powerful way to keep alumni involved in the school while also creating powerful mentoring relationships for current students?

———— 61 ————

⌖

Inquiry Is Care

It turns out that there is a profound synergy between the ethic of care and an inquiry-driven education. It starts with a simple question:

"What do you think?"

Caring for our students is more than hugging them, or being kind to them, or greeting them at the door when they come into the classroom.

Caring for our students is about listening to them. About learning about them, from them, with them. It is about understanding that if we hope to be a transformative figure in their lives, we must be willing to be transformed ourselves.

Caring for students means that we must help them fully develop their ideas and passions and habits of mind, beyond whatever a prescribed curriculum may call for. And that starts with a question—"What do you think?"—and then listening, fully and deeply, to their answer. That is the ethic of care made manifest in the inquiry process.

Asking that question—and listening deeply to the answer—is the link between the way we teach our subjects and the way we teach our children. This is how we ensure that we live the values we teach.

"What do you think?"

From Theory to Practice

- Build toward the huge open-ended question. Being asked "What do you think?" can be so scary for many of us that it's better to start with "What do you think about X?" This can give students the space they need to access the question.

- Create space for students to think about and answer this question. Create a Google form for students to write about it, pass out note cards, give kids time in groups, or make the time for one-on-one conversations with students around this question. Understand that the old teacher technique of "wait time" is hugely important here because not all students are comfortable with answering this question. Sadly, many students have been taught that their honest thoughts and ideas are not welcome in school.

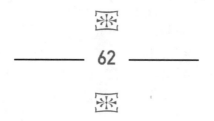

— 62 —

Schools Are Full of People

Almost every educator—ourselves included—has dealt with some kind of student behavior with a variation of the line, "Well, s/he is a kid." It makes sense, but what is interesting is that most—if not all—student behavior is a version of the same behavior in adults. And when we recognize that kids really do the same kind of things we do, it forces us to examine our own behavior in a new context, and it should lead us to create more humane schools.

First, we have to admit that our own behavior is still on that continuum. When Chris was in the classroom, it used to drive him crazy that a few of his colleagues had absolutely draconian lateness policies for kids but never handed their grades in on time. That made no sense to him. Chris was—and sometimes still is—terrible about deadlines, this book being no exception. And he was not always as fast as he would have liked to be about handing back student work. (Any former student of Chris's, reading that understatement, has just done a spit take.) So it seemed hypocritical that he'd be really strict with kids about late work. Eventually, he hit upon a policy that made sense—if you handed in work before he handed back work, he couldn't in good conscience mark it late, and if he really wanted to do something about students meeting deadlines, then he had to model it.

But the other thing that did for Chris—and what he tries to remember every day—was that it forced him to accept his own humanity and therefore accept the humanity of his students as well. We tell SLA kids who are struggling with the imperfect nature of their parents, their friends, their teachers, or themselves about one reason forgiveness is so important, simply, "I forgive other people their flaws in the vain hope that they will forgive me mine." We try to remind frustrated teachers of the same thing as well.

But it's more than just looking for forgiveness. We have to understand that we are trying to help the kids grow into the best versions of themselves. They won't be perfect. They shouldn't even try to be. We aren't. At best, we can hope that our students will be better, kinder, wiser adults than we are, but they'll never be perfect. And we'll only frustrate them and ourselves if that's the standard we hold them to.

And we worry that saying, "Well, they are kids ... " is a way to excuse their imperfection as just a function of their youth, not a function of their humanity. It serves to turn them into the other, rather than give us a moment to look at their behavior as part of the growth process we all go through. Kids miss deadlines because they are human. Kids skip class sometimes because they are human. It doesn't excuse the behavior, nor does it mean that the behavior doesn't have ramifications, but it allows us to see our students as closer to who we are. It reminds us that we should treat our students with kindness and care even when they make mistakes, because we hope that is what people will do when *we* make mistakes. And it makes it easier for students and teachers to see themselves as on the same journey of gaining wisdom.

Schools are filled with people, with all their flaws, all their beauty, and all their imperfections. And more often than we usually admit, those flaws, that beauty, and those imperfections are shared pretty closely between students and teachers.

That should be a good thing, because schools are full of people. And we are so lucky that they are.

From Theory to Practice

- Start the school year by having everyone do a strengths and weaknesses assessment. Ask students to be honest about their soft skills that are not discipline-specific. Create your own beforehand and share with them. Be honest about your flaws, and students will feel much more safe being honest about theirs.

- Make policies that recognize people's very human flaws. Zero-tolerance policies about late work or talking in class create conditions for resentment among students. Ask yourself if you want to work in a school that held you to a zero-tolerance policy for minor infractions—especially on the ones that you know are not your strengths.

——— 63 ———

⁂

Care For and About

There's more to be said on the topic of care—much more. A key for implementing an ethic of care both in the classroom and school-wide rests in two prepositions—"for" and "about." Put more pointedly, the importance of caring for, and the importance of caring about. In her seminal work *The Challenge to Care in Schools*,[53] Nel Noddings explains that a person can care *for* another individual, and that caring *about* involves the individual's ethic toward a group.

Many teachers who have played buzzword bingo in a professional development session in the last decade have heard "relationships" as the replacement, *R* in the outdated "reading, writing, and 'rithmetic." And yes, relationships are incredibly important, but they are only the start of what it means to care for our students. To care for a student, to engage in the reciprocity of a caring relationship, a teacher must develop relationships with individual students. She must connect with each student, support each student, and be energized when a successful caring relationship has been established and that student acknowledges the caring that is taking place. Caring for is difficult. It starts with a basic premise—stated perfectly by our colleague, Pia Martin—"I love you because you breathe." And its dependence on the student's being cared for to determine whether a caring relationship exists can exasperate the most seasoned of teachers. Then, of course, there are those teachers who pay no mind to whether or not their students are receiving their actions as care. These teachers will "care" the hell out of their students, not worrying about how their actions are internalized or the effects of those actions on students' perceptions of the teachers.

To care for, the person receiving the care must perceive what is happening as caring. Which is why it is both difficult and necessary.

So, too, is caring about.

Any school looking to care about also faces an uphill battle. In the age of No Child Left Behind, disaggregated data, and subgroups, we have never been so keenly aware of the multitude of options of groups about whom we can care. It could be our lowest quartile on standardized tests, our special education population, or our students receiving free and reduced-price lunch. Documentation and a bastardized notion of data provide us with any number of populations about which we may care. As many have argued, and as was a core intent of some of these reform measures, such awareness has thrown much-needed light on many of these groups.

A dynamic, caring, modern school must avoid one key pitfall. It must not see its students as members of a group based on "data." It must not perceive a group of students' needs as defined by that data. The lowest-scoring quartile of students as defined by the state reading test may, in fact, be the most struggling readers in your school, but reading may not be their problem. Let us explain.

In many schools, on the day of testing, students arrive to their assigned rooms to find the school has provided breakfast and snacks for every single student. The adults in these schools have heard that a full stomach has been shown to improve student test scores. As such, they make sure students are each fed during the ever-important testing.

Returning to our lowest-scoring quartile, we would wager that all of these students, fed a full breakfast on the day of testing, likely experienced a bump in their scores, no matter how abysmal.

When the score reports are released, though, it is rarely the first move of a school to return to the strategy of nourishing students to help them be prepared to improve their reading. Rather than providing students with meals, we take away things like art, recess, and socialization time. These, we replace with remediation and extended classes. We do this for our lowest-scoring quartile in the name of caring about them. For the remainder of the 180 school days, little attention may be paid to whether or not they are sitting through an extra ninety minutes of flat reading instruction with empty stomachs. In the next testing cycle, we will open another window of filling breakfasts for these students, and their remediation will likely bring some small improvement in the same way a person with anemia will benefit from rest in place of an influx of iron-rich foods.

Instead of this doomed routine, to care for students, let's start seeing them as individuals. When a student who has performed poorly on assignments in class makes improvements (not only when he has earned the A you know he could), take the time to write him a note letting him know you noticed the improvement.

When we take time to notice when the student who can't for the life of her keep herself seated in class advocates for herself to get a seat in the back of the room where her standing will be less of a distraction, we are caring *for*. Taking a moment to call that student's home and let the family know how impressed we were with her speaking up for herself serves only to strengthen that relationship.

Listening to understand remains as key to caring about groups of students as it is to caring for individual students. It is also just as difficult a task. In designing the schools we need, both are of critical importance.

From Theory to Practice

- Check your internal and external language about those you teach or lead. If you find yourself speaking of them as "my class" or "my faculty" without thinking of the individuals that make up those groups, it's time to push yourself to start getting to know folks as individuals.

- Acknowledge when students care for you. When students act in ways meant to care for you and what you do inside and outside of the classroom, acknowledge those moments both aloud and internally. This means the difficult moments, when you hear things that sound like student complaints, may well be their attempts to help you be the teacher you want to be. Modeling what it looks like to accept care can help our students construct the caring relationships we hope for them to have.

- Share meals. If your school allows it, ask students if they want to leave the building and have lunch at a café around the corner. If you're required to stay on campus, ask if a student wants to eat with you in the building, and offer to order food delivered. These one-on-one moments of conversation and connection will help you and your students to see each other as people first. Only then can we start building caring relations.

——————— 64 ———————

Assume Positive Intent

No matter the class size—be it five or fifty—every teacher knows the experience of walking out of the building at the end of the day and thinking, "They were out to get me today." For some, this happens more frequently than others. For some, it happens daily.

Somewhere along the line in the teaching of children, the relationship sours, and teachers lose track of the fact that they teach growing young individuals for whom both their emotions and their ability to process those emotions are still in a very formative stage.

Forgetting this key fact about the development of children can lead to another lapse of memory—that of professional perspective. This is the perspective that comes with our ability to stand back and recognize that the children are not out to get us, that none of the thousand tiny frustrations throughout our days was set in motion by students' willful intent to ruin our days.

This must be remembered if teaching is to be a sustaining profession that retains its members through the years.

To build the schools we need, we must do more than remember our students are not out to get us. We must assume positive intent.

Writing in 2008 for *Fortune*, Pepsico CEO Indra Nooyi described the benefits of assuming positive intent: "Your emotional quotient goes up because you are no longer almost random in your response. You don't get defensive. You don't scream. You are trying to understand and listen because at your basic core you are saying, 'Maybe they are saying something to me that I'm not hearing.'"[54]

Assuming positive intent in our students lets us begin to truly understand those forces driving student actions and words we would otherwise find frustrating, rather than yelling at, punishing, and alienating those students.

Assuming positive intent does not equal assuming that all students enter our classrooms and schools with the intent of learning something new or reaching some new level of academic achievement that day. Depending on circumstances, their intent may be, "I want to keep myself safe and protected." When students lack the socioemotional capacity to say these things, their actions may be to lash out and defend themselves against those around them. Assuming negative intent in these moments only leads us to compound the problem and fosters a self-fulfilling prophecy.

Assuming positive intent in these moments, asking ourselves what students may be attempting to accomplish through their actions, can help us to bring to the table the processing and reflective tools that the student may lack. Sometimes the most powerful tool is time and space away from the perceived problem. Assuming positive intent also builds a self-fulfilling prophecy that can lead students to new ways of meeting their needs that they had not known or considered possible before.

Assuming positive intent in students can be difficult in a system that does not always build up its teachers or recognize them as professionals. In such a system, teachers might assume negative intent to avoid the psychological wounds they may have suffered at the hands of the system.

To assume negative intent, though, is to further that system, to take a defensive stance that says, "I am not going to let you beat me." Assuming positive intent takes the more disruptive and proactive stance of, "I am going to listen and give you the help you need."

From Theory to Practice

- The next time a student gets all worked up in front of you, take a moment to ask what the child is trying to tell you he needs from you. Often, in these situations, we react emotionally, as though the whining student has set out deliberately to sour our mood. Instead, in these moments assume positive intent—that the student is advocating for something he needs but doesn't quite have the skills to express. From this standpoint, it is easier to reposition ourselves as teachers and display the social skills and professional practice the moment calls for.

- Assuming positive intent spreads to the adults with whom we work as well. In a faculty meeting or professional development workshop, someone will say something that is completely antithetical to what we believe is best for both children and adults. We may instinctively react in a way that assumes these folks with whom we disagree are out to destroy the lives of children and to stick to the status quo. If we pause and assume positive intent in these situations and act from a belief that these opposing beliefs are arrived at in a dedication to good, then we can try to understand why the people with whom we disagree might believe what they believe.

—————— 65 ——————

❊

Have an Excess of Good Will

We like to believe that each day teachers show up in the classroom starting with a clean slate, that the fund of good will that was depleted through one altercation with a student yesterday was replenished overnight. Unfortunately, this isn't true.

Being a teacher, being a student—these roles carry memory. The student who constantly disrupted class after repeated requests to remain on task will be remembered. The teacher who failed to take the time to ask how a student was on the day when it felt like the student's world was collapsing will be remembered. The next time a quiz grade teeters at the mercy of teacher discretion or the next time a student decides whether or not she has the drive it takes to complete a project, the ways they were treated will be remembered.

The people in schools and classrooms remember how the people in these spaces make them feel, and because of this, the schools we need must stock themselves with an overabundance of good will.

Operating with an abundance of good will means mindfully avoiding playing a "gotcha" game with students. Gotcha games in schools never teach the lessons their perpetrators believe they are teaching. The teacher who has an assignment due by a certain hour on a certain day and refuses to accept the work of a student turned in after that deadline—no matter if it is minutes, hours, or days late—will point to an important lesson about time management.

The lesson internalized by students, though, is hardly ever, "Oh, I must remember to turn things in on time." Through the experience of hard work being rejected, students are more likely to learn that *when* they do the work assigned to them matters more than how *well* they do it. The lesson becomes, "I should turn this in now, even though I haven't completed it or made something of which I can be proud."

Teachers who play gotcha games tend to be more worried about their sense of power in the classroom than they are concerned with exactly what students are learning.

Evoking the "real world" is another way to deplete good will in schools.

If teachers cite the real world as their reason for being immoveable on deadlines and persnickety about docking points for neatness or other teacherly obsessions, then they had better have made sure the content of those assignments reflected the real world as well.

Students will be more likely to meet your deadlines when the work you're asking them to do reflects the worlds from which they come and into which they are interested in going. If the realist elements of the assignments in a class are their deadlines, we have far bigger concerns at hand.

Rarely do teachers who invoke the "real world" do so in a way that includes the democracy and choice their students will find in the *real* real world.

School is real. It is difficult and confusing, and it is real. Deadlines should exist, and time management is an important skill. So too, perhaps even more so, is the giving and generating of good will. Given the choice between the citizen who has learned to submit things on time and the one who has learned the value and importance of good will, the becoming the latter is surely the higher aspiration of society.

Maintaining good will is difficult. It requires vigilance, commitment, and rejuvenation. And there is one more thing about maintaining good will: it is necessary.

From Theory to Practice

- Be realistic about deadlines. We used to explain to our students that deadlines were the last dates students could turn in work and be assured the full depth of feedback and notes on their work. We also knew that we weren't grading assignments as soon as they were turned in. So long as students got their work in before we had completed grading of other students' work in the same assignment, there was no discussion grades or points docked for tardiness.

- Avoid gotcha games. When thinking about what you need from a student, consider whether it's more important for you to see their work and help them to grow or to send them a lesson that *when* they turn in that work is more important than the actual content.

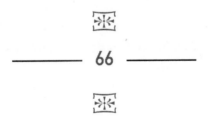

No Child Should Be On Silent

Zac was on a school visit when he received a warning from a teacher: "Don't be offended if the students don't acknowledge you if you say 'Hi' in the hallways. They're on silent and know they'll get a demerit if they acknowledge your presence." Zac was offended.

He didn't feel the offense as a cold shoulder from these middle school students. They are, after all, only following the rules, and what are schools for if not for rules?

He felt the offense on behalf of these students. At a time in their lives when norms of socialization and forging connections with others are as important as anything they're learning in math class, they'd had their legs taken out from under them with the threat of a demerit if they practice these nascent and important skills.

The silence in this school is championed by adults who claim the rule keeps the students focused. They won't be wild, crazed adolescents when they get to class if they've never get a chance to work themselves up—or so the theory goes.

It also means these students will never learn how to de-escalate themselves when they're outside the restrictive confines of the school and find themselves upset, energized, or otherwise worked up by something in life.

More important and frustrating is what policies like these teach children and say about our esteem for children. These rules are dripping with thinly veiled racism and classism. In this school, the vast majority of the students are Latino and African American; the vast majority of teachers, white. No matter how well-meaning the intent of these rules, they reflect and codify an unhealthy power dynamic.

Looking around this school, it seems no one is aware of the message of dominance and submission implicit in the rule of silence. These teachers, to a person, would likely profess their love of the children in their care and could probably list myriad ways they've worked to help students become more successful.

Creating structures in which students are silenced—rather than embracing the often difficult task of discussing social norms, answering difficult questions, and having to repeatedly model what's expected—is a cop-out of the highest order. It does students, schools, and teachers a monumental disservice.

Let's imagine how the school in our example could have been. Rather than a multitude of rules posted at every turn, students and visitors are greeted upon entry by a sign that reads, "Welcome to our community of learning."

What the visitors can't see upon entry are the frequent conversations in homeroom, advisory, or whatever the common community space is that focus on helping students articulate what a community of learning means and what it means to be a member of that community.

Rather than warning us not to be offended by not being acknowledged if we greet a student, our host encourages us to introduce ourselves to students and to let her know at the end of the day if we have any conversations that serve as particularly good models of participating in a community of learning. Then those students are acknowledged for representing the school well.

Fostering the latter kind of community takes more work than the first example. It requires adults who see themselves as authorities on helping students build community and citizenship, and it means a curriculum stocked with explicit socioemotional supports alongside academic content. At a foundational level, a school that sees itself as a community of learners must also be a place where the adults engage in frequent conversation reflecting on who they want to be and how well the school is doing at reaching this goal.

It is more work, and it is work with an eye toward equity, community, and being the better versions of ourselves.

From Theory to Practice

- Commit to the difficult conversations. If we are going to see our classrooms as the real world—if we are going to acknowledge that our children come to us with diverse pasts, headed for diverse futures, and it is our job to help them navigate those paths—then we need to be ready to listen and help students think through who they want to become. Having the difficult conversation means asking questions when our instinct might be to correct or punish. It means realizing that talking with a kid for twenty minutes might be more valuable than the thirty seconds it takes to dole out and record a demerit.

- Know you'll have those conversations many times. Few people learn a lesson the first time they encounter it. Recently we were working with a group of teachers whose students would soon have much greater access to technology in the classroom. After these teachers agreed to attempt the difficult conversation rather than punish students when they stepped out of line, Zac asked them to commit to having that conversation as many times as it took. We should definitely let students know when repeated violations of community norms are frustrating us. It's good to have authentic reactions. What we must commit to doing, though, is channeling those moments of frustration, time and again, into conversations that teach.

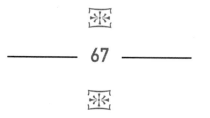

67

Audience Must Be Curated

The advent of the "read/write" Web was a boon to conversations about voice in classrooms around the country. All of a sudden, all a teacher needed to ask a student to do was to click "publish," and whatever that student had created would zoom around the world to a real audience. Will Richardson's experience blogging with his students about *The Secret Life of Bees*, for example, opened him and his students up to the world outside the classroom walls.[55]

This was a striking departure from the timeworn tradition of teacher assigns, student completes, teacher grades, repeat.

Here we were faced with the possibility that student work could make it to billions of eyes and ears. Their work mattered.

Or so the common line of thinking goes.

Audience, as it turns out, is more complicated than simply saying something (even if it is said with volume and nuance). Multitudes of trees are falling in the Internet forests, and people are there to hear them. The question is whether they make a sound when they are trying to get attention over the din of all the other falling trees.

In the schools we need, audience will be curated.

A few years ago, we asked students to select a problem in the world they thought needed solving and identify something (no matter how small) they could do to effect positive change in that problem. This was no groundbreaking assignment. It was akin to the research paper we all knew and loved.

One key difference was the realization of the possibility of audience and the need to curate it effectively. Students were choosing topics as varied as child slavery, litter in the city, and substance abuse. Even if they posted to the open class blog, there was no reason to believe they would happen into what Jean Lave and Etienne Wenger refer to as communities of practice—communities of folks engaged in the same kinds of work and ways of thinking.

The first step in our discussion of audience curation was the inclusion of metadata into students' blog posts. We examined the idea of tags on their posts and how those tags increased their visibility to outside audiences. Next, we talked about links. Because the students were accumulating many sources from many places, they were sitting on piles of data to back up their claims. Whereas the traditional paper would have them including parenthetical citations and "works cited" pages, we discussed the power of hyperlinks in helping their audience access the material they were referencing as well as increasing their visibility in Internet searches.

While these steps helped the students think about how they were crafting their messages for audience, it remained passive. It rested on the hope someone might be looking for what they were saying. The next step was jumping into the conversation. If they were talking activism, they needed to go where the activists were. We asked them to find online communities that had already formed around their topics and to take part in the conversations in those communities. It was a step toward what Lave and Wenger refer to as "legitimate peripheral participation."[56] They were connected to the work, playing at supporting their causes from the fringes rather than attempting to position themselves as experts from the start, the way a research paper asks students to do.

In addition to joining communities, students started to find other bloggers in their research who were posting on related topics. Here, too, was an opportunity to curate audience. We discussed how they might craft comments on these external bloggers' posts in ways that would establish their voices as credible and important. If they could do this, we reasoned, they would increase the rate of those bloggers' following comments back to the students' blogs. And it worked. Every day, students would share with the class that someone they'd been following and commenting on had left a comment on their posts—often with questions. This had the added benefit of legitimizing the participation.

Some of this may sound familiar to those who have had their classes send letters to the editor of the local paper commenting on a community issue. It has pieces of that exercise, but it is not that exercise. By giving students the space to have a conversation over time, curate an online presence, and cull a body of knowledge to establish a novice-level expertise, this takes a long view of establishing deeper knowledge and seeing learning as relational.

Audience curation takes time and space. It means having conversations that ask what you want to say and to whom you want to say it. It also means students must be prepared to respond to challenges to their thinking from people who may less that they are students and more that they are thinkers engaging in real-world knowledge construction. Their game must be upped.

The thing that's beautiful about all this is its contagious nature. If one assignment or project finds a real audience, then students and teachers will want to find ways for the next assignment or project to have one as well.

From Theory to Practice

- Try it yourself. Before asking students to start engaging with new communities and audiences online, think about doing so yourself for a little while. Find a blog or group of blogs about something you're interested in. It doesn't have to be education related. Then start commenting and see how the community works. This way, when you ask your students to do the same, you'll have some empathy for the process.

- Know the rules. Your school or district likely has rules in place for what information students can publish online and which spaces you can have them publish in. Before inviting students into online spaces, find out about your school's appropriate and responsible use policies.

- Shift your view. When reading and responding to student work online, read like a reader and respond as you would if you were reading the content as any interested person, not as the teacher. This new voice in responding will help students experience what it is like to have a real interactive audience and will give them a chance to see you in a new light as well.

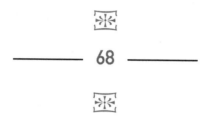

Make Better Use of the Built-In Audience

While outside audiences must be curated, there are other considerations for audience in learning and how schools can leverage them more effectively. Most specifically, students are a built-in audience, and we could be better about working with that audience.

The schools we need realize that audience is built in.

One easy way to consider this is in the English classroom, where students are frequently asked to write essays addressed to no one in particular. Even the most traditional teacher is likely, from time to time, to ask students to share their work with one another to peer edit. In technology deserts, this is usually the act of trading handwritten drafts, asking students to read what's on the pages and mark them up. In technology-rich schools, it might mean exchanging papers for editing on Google Docs or emailing a copy back and forth with comments. This is a start, but we can do better.

Simply trading papers leaves the student editor with a lack of direction. She's likely to read through, mark the most glaring punctuation errors, write "good job," and hand it back to her partner.

Without guidance, students aren't likely to get the feedback they want or need from their peer audience. They're also not likely to reflect on what that desired feedback might be. Using a more structured approach, like the writer's memo described by Jeffrey Sommers in his article "Behind the Paper: Using the Student-Teacher Memo,"[57] asks both writer and audience to think about their focus in the feedback process and what will be most helpful to the writer. In such memo writing, students pause to reflect before handing their work off to a teacher or peer editor. The memo includes a writer's thoughts on what he's created as well as specific directions for the focus and kind of feedback the writer's looking for. Rather than "Here, will you edit this?" students hand over their work with a memo that says, "I created this, and here's how I'd like you to respond."

Tools like the writer's memo take better advantage of the in-school audience than the traditional trade-and-mark approach and ask students to reflect on what they've created as well.

When students have left the editing and revising phase behind, when they feel like something they've written or produced meets their individual or class standards for published status, schools provide built-in audiences as well. For one, we can ask students to think about how to make the work useful to their intended audience rather than simply an exhibition of the skills they've been working on. The most obvious example of how audience is not considered is the use of social video sites for school projects.

In a math class, for example, the teacher may ask her students to create a video explaining the concepts taught (and, ideally, learned) during a unit of study. The students work alone or in groups to complete the assignment, then upload their videos to the designated site; the teacher reviews them, makes comments, and sends them back. In some cases the teacher might take class time to highlight some of what she has deemed as the best productions.

These videos can be made more useful. This is surely not the last time these concepts will be taught in the school. The next year or next semester, other students will follow and need to learn these concepts. However, too often the teacher will forget the video archive students have created and leave their productions to languish. Instead, leveraging built-in audience would mean realizing these new students can start their learning with the previous year's videos and use the commenting function to activate the prior students as tutors or coteachers of the content. Suddenly the videos live on, and the previous students are asked to reactivate knowledge in the service of this new audience.

Or for another example, higher-level students could review the previous year's video content and craft learning tools to help the younger students. Given the spiraling of most math curricula, this return to more fundamental concepts is likely to shore up the higher-level students' skills while providing lower-level students learning objects crafted in language divorced from the formality of textbooks.

As the Internet has opened the world up to our schools, it has become tempting to think of the world as our audience. But don't forget the audience already in our classrooms and schools. Making the best use of this audience can help to deepen knowledge and create local learning communities.

From Theory to Practice

- Connect students to students. If you teach multiple sections of the same course, create a connection across sections whereby students are peer editors for one another. They can leave work to be reviewed for one another, with specific written instructions like the memos mentioned earlier. If you teach different levels of content, you can connect sections of class for the more advanced students to be mentors to the younger students. This will create increased social capital as well as allowing you to better evaluate students' editing and revising skills.

- Keep a log of former students who had skills you know might come in handy for future students. When a current student shows a need for some help with a skill, refer to that directory and try to get those kids connected for a one-to-one tutoring session. If they video record questions and answers, see if you can use those videos as an archive of help for other students.

- Publish internally. Sadly, some schools and districts keep publishing to the outside world under a tight lockdown. This doesn't mean your students can't publish to the school. See if your school's library can catalogue student work. If so, consider setting a bar of being published to the catalog as the true mark of quality for a student.

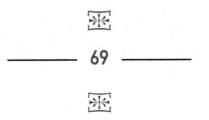

—————— 69 ——————

Parent Conferences Should Be Student Conferences

Twice each year, the folks at SLA sit down with their advisees and their advisees' parents and have a discussion of each student's progress. It's not an unfamiliar process, but the structures at SLA are different from those you're likely to have experienced in any school you've attended or taught in.

In most schools, if parents or guardians attend teacher conferences at all, students are left at home to wonder about the conclave between their parents and teachers. What about their secret lives at school is being revealed? What trouble should they brace for? Instead of an open discussion of their lives as students, these conferences can become battles for which parents and guardians, students, teachers, or all parties are woefully unprepared.

As a result, each advisor at SLA organizes conferences with their advisees slightly differently. It's another example of the importance of creating structures and then allowing room within those structures for teachers and students to make them what they need them to be.

The key was to prep our advisees as much as possible. In earlier years we told our advisees they would be responsible for leading the conference discussions, but we failed to give them adequate practice in anticipating what they might want to say and how they would make the conversations run as effectively as possible. As it turned out, many adolescents had no practice or training in how to speak to adults with agency and authority about their learning.

How would they steer their parents clear of obsessing over the one low grade to the exclusion of the other As and Bs? If the narratives and report cards fell short of their own expectations, how did they plan to reverse course in subsequent quarters?

Our time and training as teachers provide us with myriad ways to navigate these conversations, but we often leave students to fend for themselves, denying them the practice and feedback we'd allow them as they learned any other skills.

Childhood, adolescence, and schooling generally provide students with two strategies for dealing with issues that come up around their learning: "But Mom!"—and silence. Neither proves tremendously effective in fostering a discussion or ownership of learning. In "From Theory to Practice," we've outlined the approaches we've found helpful in building students' self-efficacy in conferences.

No conference is perfect. Some leave everyone involved feeling better; others, not so much. By shifting our thinking to seeing conferences as a chance to prepare students to take greater ownership of their learning rather than as an adult download of everything we've been meaning to say to parents, we move closer to seeing the potential learning in everything we do.

From Theory to Practice

Do the prep work needed to make parent conferences more useful. Here's an example of what we do at SLA:

- We showed our advisees both their report cards and narrative report cards in the advisory meetings prior to the conferences. We asked them to compare the grades on the report cards with the comments from the corresponding teachers' narratives. Sample questions: What did they notice? What surprised them? What made them feel seen? What did they want to highlight with their parents? What reactions could they anticipate, and what strategies would lead to the most productive conversations?

- Often advisees filled in a table with columns labeled, "What I want to stay the same," "What I want to change," and "How I'm going to change it."

- Looking at their report cards, their narratives, and their tables, our advisees planned the flow of their conferences. As advisors, we offered guiding questions. Would it be better for your parents to hear disappointing news earlier or later? Does it make more sense to show your report card before your narratives or the other way around? Varying parent–child relationships meant each advisee needed to plot a unique conference course.

- Once it was planned, we asked one student to volunteer for a mock conference where two other advisees played the parents. The rest of us watched. After the mock conference, the whole advisory debriefed and reflected on possible topics or situations we saw that might come up in their own conferences and how they could be approached.

- On the day of the conference, the students were the leaders. We had digital copies of the narratives and report cards, but we kept mum. The entire time, our internal monologues were some variation of *Shut up. Your only job is to support.* That's harder than it sounds.

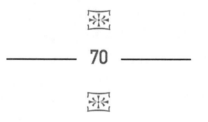

70

Communication Is Key

Speak about mobile technologies in most any school setting and you're likely to elicit a frenetic conversation about the role of these technologies in facilitating learning. You'll find educators trading app recommendations and discussing the productivity possible through mobile phones, tablets, and the like. They'll discuss things like note-taking, the dissemination of class resources, and the opportunities of all kinds of assessment.

A 2013 Pew Internet & American Life report found that 78 percent of twelve- to seventeen-year-olds have cell phones.[58] Increasingly, those are smartphones. While access to these technologies are not universal across geographies and economic statuses, the trend is clear. More and more, students are walking around with computers in their pockets.

Strangely enough, one key capability of these machines—communication—is largely absent from the conversation about using mobile technology in schools. By which we mean not communication of what they've created to new audiences, but simple person-to-person communication of messages. The schools we need must carefully consider communication ecosystems and how they can be leveraged.

The most common form of school communication to leverage possibilities is the school website. In a study published in 2008,[59] Reenay Rogers and Vivian Wright reported that parents in their study "indicated using the computer to check the school website for homework information (50.0 percent) and important school dates (55.6 percent)."

If a school is going to do one thing to communicate with parents via technology, websites are certainly the most useful tool of the moment. Considering communication between school, students, and parents from an ecosystem perspective, though, means taking account and advantage of all tools.

To begin, we must think about the messages we send and the medium best suited for those messages. Websites allow for the posting of grades, events, and news stories. Phone calls allow for longer synchronous conversations; unfortunately, these are most frequently deployed for disciplinary action. Email, which 35.8 percent of Rogers and Wright's parents reported taking advantage of, allows for asynchronous communication. Like phone calls, emails are often reserved for more lengthy and content-dense conversations. Also like phone calls, they are frequently dispatched when disciplinary issues have reached a critical mass.

As a result, most parents are likely to come to view teacher-initiated communications specific to their children as delivering bad news.

In addition to websites and email, there are other available tools we can use to create solid relationships between schools, students, and parents.

Text messages, for example, are a strong point of entry. A 2011 comScore report[60] found a 59 percent drop in web email usage among twelve- to seventeen-year-olds. On the other hand, the Pew Internet & American Life Project reported 75 percent of teens in the same age group were using texting to communicate in 2011. If schools and teachers want eyes on their messages, they must send them to the correct locations.

Texting allows faster access to students and parents. It is also an immediate tool for reporting the positive news that rarely makes it into emails. Imagine the impact on a student who's just arrived home at the end of the day on finding a text message that says, "I was impressed by your level of participation in history class today as well as the depth of your answers. Keep up the good work." Now, imagine if a similar version of that message is texted to that student's parent or guardian at the end of the work day.

Such a leveraging of communication tools would surely improve home–school relationships.

This is only one example of how schools and teachers can take an ecosystems approach to communications, and it is based on the tools of the moment. As those tools shift, approaches must adapt as well. Rather than focusing on tools, here are some questions to consider when thinking about these ecosystems:

1. What do we want to communicate with students and parents—the positive, the negative, or as complete a picture as possible?

2. What beliefs or norms will such an approach challenge, and how can we plan for resistance to these challenges?

3. What tools are our students and parents predominantly using for communication, and how can we shift into using those tools?

4. Given the speed with which these patterns and tools change, how can we plan to review our approach so that our communications are adapting as nimbly as preferences are changing?

Embarking on this process, it may be helpful to remember the importance of improving communication. In a 2002 study[61] of the impact of school community communications, Anne Henderson and Karen Mapp noted, "Family involvement that is linked to student learning has a greater effect on achievement than more general forms of involvement."

From Theory to Practice

- Celebrate the positive. In an attempt to change parents' perceptions that a phone call or other message from school can be only a harbinger of bad news, commit to contacting each student's guardian with good news at least once per quarter. Make sure each instance of good news is as detailed and worthwhile as any negative call you may normally make.

- Ask what parents prefer. If you survey students' guardians at the beginning of the year regarding their contact information, include a space where parents can include their preferred form of contact. While you may assume a phone call is best, for the parent who is heading to the graveyard shift when you're making calls, it may not be the best time. A text message, on the other hand, could be responded to on a break.

- Keep track. If you're communicating with parents and students about the positives you're seeing in class, keep a record of your communications and their content. When it comes time to offer an academic award nomination or a letter of recommendation, this log will help you to use specific examples.

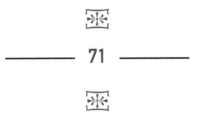

There Are No Sick or Snow Days

Each year at SLA we present a progressive pedagogy conference called EduCon (http://www.educonphilly.org). The proceeds from the conference help fund our technology program. Hosting a conference in a high school during the school year presents unique scheduling dilemmas. To avoid major nightmares, the conference takes place in late January each year. As the school is located in Philadelphia, weather at that time of the year is not always friendly.

We learned this lesson the hard way one year when, the night before the conference was to commence, the school district closed schools for the next day. This wouldn't otherwise have been a problem were it not for the fact that we invite attendees to come in during a school day and see the theory of SLA in practice. A closed school would mean no classes. No classes would mean little for attendees to do to fill their time.

We were out to dinner with friends who'd come to town early for the conference when the district made its announcement. Within minutes, our phones were buzzing with messages and calls from the student cochairs of the conference. "What do we need to do?" they wanted to know. "How are we going to get around the snow day?"

They were taking their lead from the culture of the school by immediately looking for a way to solve the problem. There are no sick or snow days. There are only "off-site" days.

The students activated the network of volunteers they'd created for the conference via texts, Twitter, and Facebook and spread the word that we were still opening the building the next day. Anyone within walking distance was welcome to make their way to the conference. The dozens of students who walked through our doors the next morning were a testament to their dedication and feelings of ownership.

This must be a fundamental component of building the schools we need. There's no need for inclement weather or sickness to delay learning or connections between students and teachers. This works in every direction.

Our colleague Paul Tritter in Boston, for example, was able to leverage free tools to keep the learning momentum going during an average snow day.

When a nor'easter struck the city, Tritter sent out a message via his course's online platform that he'd be hosting an impromptu class session for any students who could attend. The next day, more than half of his students signed on to learn.

The process wasn't without complications. The main problem Tritter faced was having to build this infrastructure on the fly; his school hadn't thought to ask how they could keep the learning open when the streets were closed. Modern schools have little excuse for being sidelined by days like these. They must plan systemically for the ability to nimbly navigate such incidents and keep connections between students and teachers active and engaging. Something as simple as a standing announcement that students can log on to school-hosted chat rooms for help with work when the building is closed can make all the difference.

This is most notably the case when school is open and students are unable to attend. At SLA, we had a high number of students who suffered from chronic illnesses that kept them from being able to physically attend school for extended stretches of time. Normally, such gaps would sideline students' learning and seem insurmountable when those students physically returned to class. Instead, our school-wide use of the open source online course management platform Moodle (we have since switched to Canvas) meant that students knew where their work would be when they were able to attend to it. This is more than what might otherwise equate to an online correspondence course; students could also email and use course chat functions to interact with their teachers and fellow students as they did their work. During periods of their lives upset by the constraints and demands of illness, we offered a chance for them to claim to some semblance of normalcy. In many instances, teachers also set up Google Hangouts or other video conferencing technologies in their classrooms, allowing students to connect in real time as they were able. They may not have been in the classroom, but they were in class.

These are the affordances of the technological world in which we live, and we can do much better at leveraging them to care for the learning of our students.

Here we would be remiss not to acknowledge that schools across the country have varying access to some of the tools that allow the kinds of connectivity just mentioned. While this truth can limit participation, it should also inspire innovation. Absent computers, class texting buddies can help to form partnerships for students to collaborate on classwork and create a sense of community in which students know there is at least one person in the class to whom they can turn if they are absent or simply need some clarification on an assignment. Where texting isn't an option, teachers can host free conference call tutoring sessions via a number of online services where students can call in with questions outside of class time. Many of these ideas we mention here, we learned from the pioneering work of our friend Brian Crosby, who made sure that a student of his with cancer did not miss class.[62] Anyone interested in delving deeper into this idea should seek out his writing.

We live in a connected society. The question, "How am I going to catch up?" after a snow or sick day should be obsolete. Instead, the new question must be, "How are we going to keep learning?"

From Theory to Practice

- Plan for the worst. Consider the weather or the needs of your students who are absent from school for prolonged periods of time for excused and extenuating reasons. As a faculty, brainstorm what it would take to keep the learning during these periods as uninterrupted as possible. From there, you've got a list of requirements for an online learning management system (LMS). There are hundreds of products online. It's best to have this list to help you do your research and see which product actually fits your need and your budget.

- Make learning mobile before you need to. During the snowstorm, our students were able to leverage mobile platforms because the school used those platforms to communicate information when emergencies weren't happening. It should be not the exception, but rather the standby. Students who were chronically ill didn't have Canvas set up just for their illnesses; it was the online space where they'd already learned that all their learning materials and resources could be found.

- Start small if need be. If an entire LMS sounds like it's just too much, choose one channel. Maybe you need a school Twitter account as the first step. Maybe each curricular department sets up a standing "office hours" online chat through a free service. Whatever the access point, it's not necessary to build the entirety of your technology infrastructure at once. Know your needs, know your capabilities, and build from there.

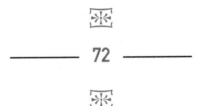

Get Rid of the Pencil Lab

Where was your school's pencil lab?[63]
Think hard on the question. Where was the room set aside with rows upon rows of desks equipped with freshly sharpened #2s and a teacher whose express objective was to help you learn the proper implementation of pencil-based technology so that, say, your math teacher could attempt to integrate pencils into her lesson?

When did your English teacher announce that he'd reserved the school's pencil lab so that you could go down and do some word processing using your school's new install of graphite?

"Computer labs" should be as ridiculous sounding and backward as the image of a pencil lab.

The pencil hit the market and, with the exception of a few lessons in handwriting, we never really looked back.

Thinking of the dangers implicit in putting these technologies in the hands of students—hand cramps, dangerously pointed ends—it boggles the mind that pencils and pencil 2.0 (pens) weren't banned outright by school boards across the country. From the first moments, they were surely being put to all sorts of nefarious purposes. Social networking must have skyrocketed with the instant messages passed around class with their "yes" and "no" checkboxes—and what about the hurtful, harmful, and hateful memes about one another that could be spread around schools?

We would have liked to be in on the professional development organized by schools and districts to help teachers get on board with pencils. Everyone groggily sitting in the cafeteria, sucking down industrial-strength coffee, mumbling to one another how the pendulum had swung once again to another edu-fad.

How many schools were kept from doing really interesting things by cadres of teachers who sidestepped their own learning by admitting freely that they were "pencil-illiterate" or "pencil-phobic"?

And when the pencils had been worn down to the nubs by early adopters who saw these technologies for the freedoms they represented—enthusiasts who crowded the pencil labs before and after school so that they might push these pencils to their furthest limits—what happened then? Surely we fretted about having to spend money on pencil upgrades—again. We wonder how we answered the administrator who questioned why students and teachers couldn't just make do with the pencils we'd bought a few years ago.

So let's ban the phrase "computer lab" and instead focus on how to embrace the current and future technology the way we embraced the pencil.

From Theory to Practice

- Create access. If your students and teachers need to get on a list, go to a separate room, use a locked-down version, or overcome any other hurdle to get to the technology they want and need to learn creatively, then you have built a system designed to keep that technology out of their hands. Instead, think about what you can do to build a system that puts those devices in the hands of kids, on the off chance that they could create something or produce something representative of their learning.

- Claim literacy. Rather than designating one or two individuals in your school as the "tech people" or "techie teachers," do whatever you can to own that label. If you stand in front of any room of people and claim you "just don't get technology," you've done a great deal with those few words to grant others permission to stop learning about new and powerful tools.

- Plan for updates. A grant might get you the devices you want and your students can use. What, though, are you doing to make sure those devices are replaced when they reach old age? What room are you carving into your budget now to make sure students are able to build and produce tomorrow?

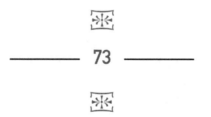

73

Technology Must Be Ubiquitous

Technology must be everywhere in schools. A one-to-one person-to-device ratio can no longer be optional. Today's world is both analog and digital, and often it is both of those things at the same time. It cannot be seen as a luxury to provide students with the digital tools of the modern world. And it is not OK to consider giving children a laptop as something that will preclude other profound instruments of learning. As Gary Stager said at the first EduCon, "We are the richest nation in the world. We can provide our children with a computer *and* a cello."[64]

And once we have provided students with the devices, we must make sure they don't stay in the backpack. Ubiquitous technology means that they are pulled out in the hallways, they are used in lunchrooms, and they are used in classrooms. When technology is used only when the teacher says so, it remains special, different, and therefore not intrinsic to the learning that our kids do.

But when it is ubiquitous, it becomes a part of who we are and how we learn. That is the pathway to helping students understand the world in which they live. When it is ubiquitous, students learn how to put it away when they want to or need to. When it is ubiquitous, it is no longer special. That is the moment when we stop worrying about integrating technology and start concerning ourselves with learning.

From Theory to Practice

- Stop anticipating. In some classrooms, teachers view digital devices as containing a finite set of useful functions. As such, they tell their students when they will and will not need to bring those devices to class. Stop doing that. To keep technology out of the classroom because what you planned won't require technology is to preclude the serendipity of discovering new resources or the need for students to build new resources to share. Such actions also make it seem as those the technology is exotic to you and you don't see it as part of moving through the day the way many students and teachers have come to understand it.

- Ask for suggestions. What ideas do your students and your colleagues have for how a piece of technology could be useful in a given moment of learning? If you don't know, it's time to ask. Some of the best lessons will erupt when you turn from your lesson plan and toward your class to say, "What could we do with this?" You won't think to ask the question until you allow the technology to be ubiquitous.

74

Technology Must Be Necessary

This seems like an easy one. It is hard to think of a part of American life that is not touched by technology today outside of our schools. And yet, most students, teachers, and administrators today do not feel that a laptop or a tablet is absolutely necessary to their success inside of school. Over 68 percent of American households have broadband Internet at home.[65] But for some reason, we continue to expect kids to dutifully take notes in an analog fashion and cut themselves off from the world outside the classroom walls.

It is time to admit that technology must be a necessary component of learning in school. Let's use something as simple as note-taking as an example. Why would we make students handwrite notes in a classroom anymore? Today, when students have the ability to use a tool like Evernote or Google Docs, notes can be compiled, reorganized, and shared synchronously or asynchronously. The ability to filter and the ability to search means that students can reference and use their notes more quickly and powerfully than before. That doesn't mean that every note has to be taken online—in fact, Chris enjoys using the Evernote moleskin to take notes the old-fashioned way and then digitize them—but the idea that students could create an electronic repository of their notes, their ideas, and their work should not be revolutionary anymore. It should simply be done.

But that is just the low-hanging fruit. Technology is necessary for reasons far greater than being a better way to take notes or write a paper. Technology is necessary in our schools because it allows our students to see that their work is authentic in the world. No longer is student work simply a one-to-one dialogue between teacher and student. Students can publish their work and take part in communities of practice both inside and outside of their immediate school community. And students can see that their work is adding to the larger dialogue about topics of importance to them. The first time a student at SLA received an email from someone asking a follow-up question about a project, his vision of himself as a scholar completely changed. Every time students see their videos make the rounds on Twitter, they understand they have created a vision of the world that is shared. When students use social media to reach out to experts in their fields, students develop their ability to inquire deeply and interact with adults who are further along on that path of inquiry. When students use technology in a science classroom to do powerful experiments or in an engineering class to make their ideas become real, students no longer are only learning science and engineering; they are becoming scientists and engineers.

Technology becomes necessary when students see it as vital to the way they learn, when they cannot imagine doing the work without it. It is necessary when it allows them to do things, learn things, create things, and share things like never before. Technology becomes necessary when it makes the work students do more authentic, more empowering and shared to the world. And isn't that how we as educators want our students to view the artifacts of their learning? Technology is necessary not just because it is vital to the lives our students—and our society—lead outside of school. It is necessary because it can be married to progressive pedagogy and used to help students become fully realized scholars of the world.

From Theory to Practice

- Stop doing it the other way. When SLA started, our online LMS was barely a shell. Still, within it was a course to which all faculty were subscribed. Within that course was a discussion forum called "Staff Planning." In that forum you could find every pertinent piece of news and discussion, from early planning days to what was to happen on the latest early dismissal day. Staff were expected to check in on the discussion forum and contribute. Email had a way of getting deleted, and messages were owned only by senders and recipients. The forum allowed for a democratic, archival, and necessary space for getting information in the school. We knew we needed it because it had been made the way things got done.

- Stop buying other stuff. A school moving to a one-to-one program announced they'd not be buying paper planners for all of their middle school students. All of a sudden, the calendar abilities of the students' devices became necessary. First, though, the school had to be willing to see the traditional way of doing things as no longer necessary. This shift can be uncomfortable, and it will push thinking forward.

- Stop treating tech as "other." Let the students take out their laptops even when—especially when—there's not a teacher-directed reason to use it. Kids will find ways to incorporate it into the work they are doing in ways the teachers didn't anticipate. And yes, they might use it inappropriately every now and then too. That's OK. Kids still pass notes in class, too.

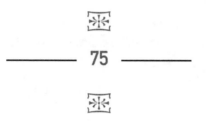

Technology Must Be Invisible

In most schools, whenever the laptop cart is wheeled into a classroom, we say the kids are doing a "technology project." But to say that is to miss the point. Just because a student uses a laptop or a tablet or some other piece of equipment that is new-ish to do their work does not mean they are doing a technology project.

It means they are doing their work.

Until we stop fetishizing technology by making it the focal point of the work every time we pull it out of the closet, we will never move past the notion of "technology integration" to a place of "modern learning." (We're not so hot on its living in a closet, either.)

The idea that technology must be invisible in school is simply this: Using technology to inquire, to create, to share, to research, to learn is not and should not be notable anymore. It should simply be a matter of course.

Using technology in school is not the point—learning is.

When technology becomes invisible, students take more ownership of their use of technology. When students use a combination of books, internet research, and expert interviews to do a deep dive into a topic, technology is not the focus; research and inquiry are.

When a teacher says, "OK, let's get into our groups," and one student opens up a Google Doc and three other students move their chairs, we can see a moment when the technology is not the focus; collaboration is.

When students are doing presentations and rather than seeing thirty PowerPoints we see PowerPoint, Prezi, videos, and old-fashioned poster board, but no matter what medium the presentation takes, students have a personal sense of aesthetic value and how to use a visual medium to communicate an idea, then technology is not the focus; the idea and the quality of the presentation is.

That is how technology becomes invisible—when it becomes like the very oxygen we breathe. We don't think about it every minute, but it is always there and always vital.

This doesn't mean we never talk about technology, by the way. There are still moments when we learn about the technology itself, and that's a good thing. Whether it is in a computer science class where students are learning to program, or in a technology infusion workshop where we help students to learn how to fully integrate the technology into their sense of themselves as a student and citizen, there are moments when we—students and teachers—make the invisible visible. Much as we have to be thoughtful about airflow when we build physical structures and machines, we should be thoughtful about technology when we build learning spaces and learning experiences. And both students and teachers should have moments of reflection of how the tools affect the learning. But there's a big leap between understanding how the tool is both vital and transformative to the work and making the work always about the tool.

When technology becomes invisible in a school, learning becomes the focus. That should always be our goal, regardless of the tools we use to get there.

From Theory to Practice

- Anticipate needs. An elementary school excited about the delivery of tablet computers that would be coming to each classroom held a staff meeting. A teacher raised her hand. "Where will we be charging these?" Silence. While the administration had been thrilled to procure the devices, they had not anticipated what it would take to keep them running, to store them securely. In other words, they had insured the technology would be visible, notably as a problem to be solved. By anticipating the needs of immediate technology purchases and building spaces to accommodate new and next-generation purchases, we've done the groundwork of making technology invisible.

- Check the oxygen levels from time to time. When walking around your learning space, is everyone using technology in fully engaging and productive ways? Are there rooms where it is noticeably more difficult to breathe in the tech use? If so, perhaps it's time to ask how you can better meet the learning needs of your faculty and staff. Invisible technology is part of the business of learning. It isn't technology that's *literally* invisible because people haven't gotten the learning and play time necessary to feel comfortable using it.

———— **76** ————

꘎

Class Blogs Should Be Open Spaces

The walled discussion board almost feels normal at this point. As a tool, we can understand the use of a discussion board as a community builder and idea incubator. We are fans of those concepts.

While it is still frustrating when discussion boards are used for awkward or inauthentic purposes, we can see their usefulness as an archive of correspondences for an online community. On SLA's online LMS, all community members have access to a discussion forum—SLA Talk—that's been live since the school's first year. New freshmen are part of the fold, and their thoughts intermingle with those of the first graduating class when they were freshmen. It's readable, documented institutional memory. An observer is just as likely to find a thread discussing student language use in the hallways as they are to find a debate about the latest video game release. It is a simple artifact of community online.

Students and courses can also use school-provided blogs, and we've seen them used in vastly different ways. In one instance, a few students are assigned to post their thoughts each week on the reading leading up to that week's class. Each student is required to reply to one post per week, with the option of passing on one week during the semester. While the thinking in these posts might be top-notch, it rarely gets discussed in live class conversation.

In another instance, each person is encouraged to post weekly. The posts' content might be related to the readings or simply to the topic for the week. No replies are required, and the posts are regularly referenced by the teacher in discussion.

If blogging is to be required for a course, the latter instance comes closest to ideal practice—not required, but preferred; not for nothing, but tied to class.

In both instances, class blogs live within the walled garden. The thoughts with which teachers and students play will never find footing in an RSS (Real Simple Syndication) reader or enjoy comments from those who have reading lists contrary to those on a given class syllabus.

Comments and commenting should be public. Comments from anyone around the globe should be invited and allowed. Students' thoughts should mingle in the cyber-ether. A teacher should moderate comments, certainly, when helping students to play David Perkins' "junior version of the game."[66]

Commenting should be open to the public for two reasons. One, the refinement of thinking benefits from a plurality of opinions, and the Internet offers a cacophony that challenges students to sculpt and refine their thinking in ways impossible to imagine.

Two, an open class blog asks students to clear their throats and use their public voices while connected to a class setting in which they can find support when their voices are challenged. Students are likely to experience pushback when posting in this space. Such experiences are difficult to take early on. They ask students to defend and explain their thinking in complex ways often impossible for a single classroom teacher to handle. Sure, kids want people to read what they post, but they never expected people to disagree with their thinking.

Opening their blogs gives students the chance to write with a cohort of support while enriching the experience and exposing them to the democracy of thinking on the Web. Walling off a class blog runs the risk of students taking their opinions into the world untested and unprepared for criticism. It also robs them of the practice microphone that a class blog could and should become.

From Theory to Practice

- Know your community. Each school or district will have its own appropriate/responsible use policy. Most of these policies discuss student interactions and access to online posting environments. Make it your business to know yours, and, if you find it to be too closed off from the outside world, to advocate for its amendment.

- Know the law. There are two federal laws that you should be aware of before working with students and student information online. The Family Educational Rights and Privacy Act (FERPA)[67] and the Children's Online Privacy and Protection Act (COPPA)[68] should be mandatory reading for anyone interested in what they can and cannot publish about students online.

- Ask the students. So often, teachers will tell students what they are to publish online. It might be a homework assignment or an update on classes. Instead, take the unexpected tack of asking your students what they might want to create to go in online spaces. You might end up explaining video games, reviewing popular culture, or something else not specifically outlined in your district curriculum—but chances are that writing is of a type called for in the curriculum.

——— **77** ———

⊠

Make Personalization Authentic

There is a lot of talk in ed-tech and ed-reform about personalization right now. There are a lot of folks on the vendor floor at national conferences who will sell you products that supposedly personalize learning, and much of the buzz around something like Khan Academy is that it personalizes the learning for kids.

We should be careful about how we use that term, and we should be very skeptical of how well computerized programs can really personalize learning for kids. Most of what we see—especially from curriculum and assessment vendors—involves personalization of pace while still maintaining standardization of content. That's not good enough. While a program that allows you to take a pretest and then get practice problems and tutorials and videos that are specifically tailored to the things you did poorly on and allows you to practice those things until you can pass the test (a) might raise test scores and (b) might be marginally better than a "traditional" classroom that did not offer choice of content or pace (and we put "traditional" in quotes because legions of teachers have been giving kids real choice for decades), that doesn't mean we should settle for that. We'll even grant that these programs have a place in helping students to master the concepts that someone else tells them (and us) they have to learn—and to that end, SLA uses one of these programs to help kids get ready for the state exams—but let's not call it personalized. Here's why.

First, this notion of personalization of learning removes student choice from learning what they most want to learn. It still assumes that kids have to learn everything we want them to learn. We don't know how, in this era of high-stakes tests and corporate education "reform," in which test scores are the profit-and-loss statements for schools, we can get away from this systemically, but we have to. And because language matters, we don't think we should call self-paced tutorials real personalization. (It also isn't necessarily anything new. The old Scholastic Reading Aptitude [SRA] learning modules did much the same thing in the 1970s; they just weren't computerized.) We have to get to a place where we understand that, while there are skills and content that students do need to at least be exposed to, these "must haves" are probably far more expansive than they need to be right now. They are being taught at the expense of all kinds of other things that students could do, create, and learn that would ignite their passion and their minds in ways that mandated content consumption doesn't.

Second, this model of "personalization" is still building off of a deficit model in which students are steered away from doing the things they are good at so they can focus on the things they are bad at. We have to move to a system where we create more space for students to play to their strengths while mitigating their weaknesses. Instead, we create system after system where kids are told to keep working on the things they are worst at. And then we wonder why kids don't like school—or worse, think they don't like learning.

Finally, too much of this model of "personalization" misses another highly personal piece of learning—the artifacts of learning we create when we learn. Students should be able to own their learning by creating stuff that matters to them. At SLA, we have seen students build biowalls, make movies, apply complicated mathematical concepts as they built trebuchets and robots, write and enact public action campaigns, and form book clubs around genre studies of their own definition. All of these examples are mapped to standards, all of these are ways for students to demonstrate mastery of the same concepts that we test on, but in ways that are truly personal to the student, because they choose them. That's the model of personalization we want to see schools move toward.

From Theory to Practice

- Examine choice. Much of personalized learning touts choice. Evaluate this claim by asking whose choice students are making. If they are choosing one of a set of preplanned computerized choices or even from a limited list of teacher choices, then that's not real choice. Build assignments for students that take learning as their goal, and provide students with the room to design and advocate for the choice of how that learning will be made manifest.

- Open the calendar. If students are choosing how they show their learning, it stands to reason that showcasing will happen on varied timelines. Set a deadline for when all submissions must be turned in and work with students individually to identify where in the calendar they'd like their individual product be completed.

- Use the other offerings for what they're good for. If you have web access, it makes sense for your students to turn to sites like Khan Academy when they need another voice or medium for understanding content. When using these resources, avoid the danger of making them a lesser stand-in for deeper learning and teaching.

─────── 78 ───────

⌖

Ask Better Questions

I n 2013 the Providence Student Union published the results of
an experiment they had conducted.[69] They gave fifty successful
adults a math test based on the sample New England Common
Assessment Program (NECAP). Rhode Island uses the NECAP
as a high-stakes test in which students must achieve at least a
"Partially Proficient" ranking to graduate from high school.

As the results show, apparently you don't need to be considered partially proficient to be successful:

> Four of the 50 adults got a score that would have been "profi-
> cient with distinction," seven would have scored "proficient," nine
> would have scored "partially proficient," and 30—or 60%—would
> have scored "substantially below proficient." Students scoring in
> the last category are at risk of not graduating from high school.[70]

Now, some folks will say that the adults didn't have the time to
study for the test, but that isn't the point. The point is that these
successful adults were no longer proficient in the math skills on
the test because they did not use them in their day-to-day lives.
And yet, Rhode Island has mandated "Partially Proficient" as a
graduation requirement for students starting in 2013.

Why?

If we are to have mandatory graduation exams, let's base them on the skills that adults need in their world. What would happen if we asked successful adults what math they actually use day-to-day? Do most people use the quadratic equation, or do they need the math skills that allow them to create budgets for their business, calculate interest rates on their mortgages, or understand polling data in the *New York Times*?

That doesn't mean we shouldn't teach skills beyond what may show up on a graduation exam. What it means is that we have to start asking ourselves better questions about what skills are necessary for a high school diploma. And we need to start asking better questions of our students in their schoolwork and on the tests we require them to take.

From Theory to Practice

- Anticipate the challenge. Students may not always ask that fateful question, "When am I going to need this?"—but the chances are pretty good they're thinking it. When drawing up unit and lesson plans, think about your answer to that question. If the answer is not immediately apparent, think deeply. If a concept's only reason for being taught is its listing on a curriculum guide, then teaching has jumped the rails.

- Don't know the answer. Ask students questions to which you're unsure of the answers. When we ask students only those things about which we are certain, they can smell it on our breath. Instead, find ways of looking at well-worn information that ask students to try new things, to make them obsolete, and to explain them to new audiences.

—— **79** ——

⁂

Cocurate Your School

Most classrooms have bulletin boards. It's where teachers put up exemplary work—often ten or twenty versions of the same project. And many teachers hang up projects in the hall-ways. We do that too, but does it go far enough? What if students and teachers treated their school as a living gallery and made more deliberate attempts to curate the school?

We didn't set out to do that at SLA, but that's what has hap-pened. Over the past few years, students had ideas about creating murals or taking over pieces of the school to display their work. Teachers have taken entire walls to do permanent installations, and we've even taken over the walls of the city outside our school for art installations.

The result is that our school is slowly transforming, wall by wall, to be a showcase of the work and planning and thoughtfulness of the people of SLA. It happened because of an overwhelming desire to say yes to good ideas, rather than a deliberate attempt to say, "Every teacher must take over a twenty by twenty foot space outside their classroom," which probably would have led to disaster.

Instead, we now have a dedicated space for a rotating gallery of student art work. We have an original mosaic of a Philadelphia cityscape hanging on the third floor. The space outside the fifth floor math lab is now filled with unique, student-generated equations and formulas. There are original biowall structures throughout our hallways. Every year, masks from our Spanish 4 class take over the back wall of the second floor. Walls are being repurposed as canvases. Ceiling tiles are being redesigned. It's exciting. The school—always a colorful place—is now really becoming our own.

And now that it has happened organically, we are having to actually step back and think about what it might look like moving forward. A group of underclass students are going to take the art gallery over from the seniors who started it. Teachers and students are now beginning to collaborate on spaces more deliberately. The school is becoming our gallery. It is exciting to watch.

And as with many things that have happened at SLA over the years, this has evolved out of a fundamental belief that students should do real things that matter and that our job, as the adults, is to support rather than to control. And as has happened in the past, we are reverse engineering the questions in "From Theory to Practice" to ask ourselves about our public spaces as we move forward.

What would happen if all of us treated our schools as galleries to be cocurated by students and teachers? How might we transform the way we think about learning?

From Theory to Practice

If you are moving to a community-curated space, consider working with the students to answer the following:

- What is the process by which the community changes our public spaces?
- How does this enhance the way we live in our spaces?
- Is this a permanent installation that will stay as is? Or will the space change?

- If this installation changes or needs care, who cares for it? Who curates it?
- How can we use the space as a teaching tool for ourselves? For others?

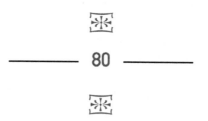

Organize

So the question before us is, "How do we effect change?" For folks arguing for a more humane, more inquiry-driven, more citizenship-minded, more modern education, it can be daunting. The forces that seem to be working against this kind of education are many. We are outspent by those who argue that workforce-driven, test-measured education is what we really need in this country. Worse, it appears that the very language of our best ideas is often co-opted by those who, in the end, are creating a very different kind of schooling from what our best ideas are really about.

And the traditional advocates for public schooling—teachers unions—are caught in a fight that, while linked to the kind of issues that affect modern schooling, are not the same. While workers' rights, collective bargaining, teacher evaluation, or any of the other issues facing teachers are incredibly important, historically, unions have not been the drivers of pedagogical change.

What we need now is a new kind of organization—one that unites teachers, students, parents, and administrators who all believe that school can be more powerful than it is now. This may not be a national organization at first. Maybe this will happen district by district, school by school. Maybe the time has come for fewer "Education Nation" moments, and more town halls.

We are living in a time when there is a national movement with incredible wealth arguing for a vision of education that seems to ring false for many of the people who are walking the walk in schools. Perhaps the answer is to win the argument on a different stage—the hyperlocal stage. And with social media and the speed of communication, is there any doubt that those arguments could spread?

What if in cities and towns all over the country we saw parents and educators (who are often the same people, it should be noted) and students and community members come together to discuss their best vision of what they hope school to be? What if, rather than the rhetoric of "fixing broken schools" that we hear so often from the edu-corporate reform movement, we had a grassroots movement articulating our best ideas for what we hope a modern education could be? And what if we actually all worked together to make those dreams real?

Maybe that's what we need—hyperlocal, globally networked organized groups of citizens who believe that inquiry-driven, project-based modern schools are better than what we have today.

From Theory to Practice

- Set the table. Schedule a local meeting space (library room, classroom after school), and invite that handful of folks with whom you've engaged in conversations about what school can be. From there, see where people want to go. What would they like to create? What are they currently working on? Whatever it is, don't let anyone leave without committing to a next step.

- Connect online. There is likely a parent group or a singular parent near you who is using social media to speak out about what they think schools should be. Find them, and start a conversation. Sometimes the actions we are looking for must be built upon the conversations we still need to have. Finding folks online and working toward a common cause is that first step.

- Set audacious goals. It doesn't mean set unreasonable goals, but shoot the moon. Dream big about what you believe a school or a learning community can be. If we don't dream big for our kids, we'll end up congratulating ourselves that we painted the classrooms a better color, and little else.

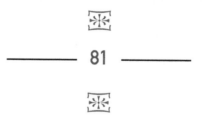

81

Teach Thoughtfulness

Once we accept the premise that the purpose of school is to help our students become fully realized citizens of a modern world, we have to ask ourselves: What are the universal traits of the modern citizen?

We want people who are thoughtful.

Not "thoughtful" as a synonym for "nice." Our world needs people who are truly "full of thought."

There has long been an anti-intellectual thread to American society, and sadly, school has probably done as much to perpetuate it as it has to eliminate it. By catering to the "right answer" and reinforcing curricular decisions that teach kids in a top-down, "We know what is best to learn" fashion, we have long sent the message that thoughts that are outside the prescribed canon—and therefore kids who are outside the prescribed canon—are not OK.

When we treat our classes as lenses on the world, not walled-off silos, we allow students to make connections to other ideas in a way that will allow them to connect idea to idea, thought to thought, in ways that can be never-ending.

When we honor our students' ideas and dare them to push those ideas further, we teach students that the world of ideas is a place where they can live.

When we model thoughtfulness by deconstructing our own ideas in public, we teach our students that thoughts are not fixed, final, and perfect, so that students can understand how reflective practice can lead us to deepen our ideas.

When we are open as teachers so that student ideas can influence and change our own ideas—so that we are learners in our own classrooms—we teach students that authority has no monopoly on ideas, on "right." A teacher who is willing to say to a student in a classroom, "I never thought about it that way" opens a child up to the power of their own ideas to influence others, and that is an invaluable lesson to learn.

And when we create an inquiry-driven, project-based curriculum, in which students can take the ideas of the classroom, make them their own, go deeper into the ideas that most speak to them, and then build artifacts that reflect their ideas and the path they traveled to develop them, we let students see the power of their ideas made manifest in the world.

In the end, the hallmark of a great school isn't the number of our ideas, facts, and thoughts that our students remember at the end of four years; rather, it is the number of ideas, facts, and thoughts they discover for themselves that built on the foundations we helped them to build. A test can never measure this, and we have to do it anyway.

From Theory to Practice

- Give space to explore. In your lesson and unit plans, carve out space that is specific to exploration. It can be of given content, or it can be of content procured by the students. The goal is to give students the place to wonder about something and capture those wonderings in some form. It might be an online notebook, it might be a sketchpad, it could be an audio recording. Carve out space for students to explore and then ask them what they found. Take that as your cue to explore as well.

- Seek advice from the experts. When designing a learning plan, don't work in solitude. Turn to those who will know more about the effectiveness of your plan than you ever could. Ask the students. It could be a random rotating team of current students to whom you present a unit plan, asking, "What do you think?" Or you could recruit former students and say, "Here's what we did when you were in the class. What would make it better?" Either way, seek real input from those charged with learning in your class. A survey now and then can be helpful. True focus-group-like conversations, though, can be invaluable.

——— 82 ———

⊞

Teach Wisdom

We think of wisdom as something that comes only with time. Traditionally, the young person is considered headstrong, while the elder is wise. Societally, we think of wisdom as being hard-earned—and interestingly, it is often gained by those who are not considered "good at school." It is the stereotype of the elder who learned at "the school of hard knocks," and not something that we traditionally think of when we think of high school students. When a young person actually displays these traits, we say they are "wise beyond their years."

And yet, if we are to help students to become fully realized citizens during their time with us, it is essential that we help them to develop "soundness of action" and "good judgment"—in other words, wisdom—during their time with us. Because without the wisdom to apply those ideas thoughtfully, intellect and knowledge can be profoundly dangerous.

So then, wisdom becomes about decision making and action taking, but the accumulation of wisdom is about reflection. Wisdom is about understanding that "doing" is not the end of the learning process; reflecting on what we have done is. Wisdom is about learning from your mistakes, but then being able to apply those lessons not only so that you do not make the same mistakes again, but also so you can foresee and forestall mistakes before they happen.

Wisdom also means not falling so in love with your own ideas that you cannot see the unintended harm those ideas could do, or cannot see the potential in someone else's possibly conflicting ideas.

In the end, our willingness to engage in reflective practice with our students, our dexterity in creating the conditions for students to engage in real work that matters, and our ability to help them see themselves and that work in the context of the never-ending stream of human history—in short, our ability to help our students to become more wise—is the most important thing we can do. If our students can learn from their experiences with us, while they still have a safety net, we will have enabled them to make better decisions about their own lives when they leave our walls. And if we have helped them to be more thoughtful and wise about the world around them, then we have helped them become better citizens of the world at large.

From Theory to Practice

- Do real stuff. We have to dare kids, help kids, and support kids to attempt great things, struggle, reflect, learn, and try again. That is the cycle through which wisdom is gained. But we rarely reflect on the things we do not care about. When kids are engaged in work that matters to them, work that is authentic and has real meaning, we create the conditions for students to reflect and gain wisdom. The coach who has students watch game footage and critique their own performances, both individually and as a team, is doing more to help her students become more wise than is the teacher who covers the content of a world history class at a blistering pace.

- Be scholar-activists. It isn't enough to do real work that matters. We have to help students see that work in the context of the work that has gone on before us. That is why it is important not just to study history but to develop the tools of the historian. When our students see themselves as scholar-activists, they place their actions in the stream of human history, and they can learn from the mistakes of the past while they endeavor to take action in the present.

- Be willing to live in the soup. Life is messy, and there are few absolutes. When we own that publicly with our students, we encourage them to come with us on our own journeys of figuring things out. In a conversation on Twitter, Bill Ferriter wrote, "Learning only happens when there is tension between what kids think they know and what they see in the world around them."[71] And he is right. It is in that moment of conflict between what we think we know and what we experience that meaning happens. We need to help our students understand that we—all of us—are forever engaged in what Alvin Toffler said was the process of learning, unlearning, and relearning.[72] And our students will be far more willing to listen to that message if we model ourselves.

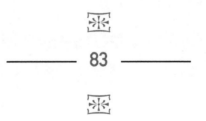

83

Teach Passion

One critique of this generation of young people is that they are apathetic, but in our experience with the students we meet both in and out of SLA, the critique is no more apt for this generation than for our own or those before us. The young women and men we teach are looking for a reason to care about more than what society is telling them is important. They are looking for a reason to be more than the stereotype of youth culture that is portrayed through mass media.

We have to ask ourselves how often school gives them that reason.

In most schools, the things students care most about are extracurricular—sports, drama, newspaper, marching band, debate—and students across the country endure class solely for the right to participate in the things they actually care about. When we were both coaches, we knew we had students who were keeping their grades up for the right to play and little else, and every coach we've known has similar stories. And while we weren't against using eligibility as a way to motivate an athlete, we have to ask—Why is this OK? Why is it OK to tell students to endure seven hours of classes and two or three hours of homework so they can enjoy an hour or two of the activity they are most passionate about?

The thing is, the "soft" lessons we most want to teach are there to be learned in extracurricular activities. Watch an athlete run sprints to train for the season, or the lead in a play work a scene for hours, or the editor of the school newspaper edit article after article—this isn't just about "fun," this is about passion.

Yet we partition off all of the work they do on these subjects to the world of extracurricular rather than searching for the curricular connections they most need. If you think an understanding of algebra and geometry is absent from the sports field, you haven't been paying attention. If you are not mining the importance of close reading in the staging of a drama or musical, you're choosing to turn a blind eye. If the drive to edit, revise, repeat is not readily apparent in the publication of each issue of the school paper, look again.

Schools can be places of great passion where students learn what it means to be scholar-activists, fully invested in authentic work that matters to them today, not someday.

When we do this, we will fully realize the promise of the idea that school should not just be preparation for real life; rather, school can be real life—not just after school, but all day long. Students and teachers can together make meaning relevant to the lives we all are leading now, as well as growing thoughtfully into the lives we will live tomorrow.

From Theory to Practice

- Make it relevant. If we cannot help students to see how what they are learning in our classes is relevant to their lives, then how can we ask the overwhelming majority of our students to develop a passion for what we teach? And while there will always be a percentage of our students who fall in love with our subject because of its beauty or intrinsic interest, that's not good enough. It is the difference between teaching *Hamlet* primarily through the literary structure devices Shakespeare uses or using it as a text to examine how our own human struggles are part of a continuum of hundreds of years of struggle to make meaning of our lives.

- Make it real. Have students create real artifacts of their own learning that have an impact in the world. High school students can create public service campaigns for their neighborhoods around environmental/scientific issues. Students can create documentaries and submit them to film festivals. Students can debate the meaning of historical events and the impact they have on our society today. They can do fieldwork science, getting out of the laboratory and doing field research in the world at large. And students can engage in all manner of engineering projects, from building apps to building small-scale solar installations. And in all these examples, make sure that students are not just asking the questions we have given them, but also asking and answering their own questions, building knowledge and meaning from their own line of inquiry.

- Make it live in the world. Whether through leveraging the Web, creating opportunities for performance, or simply creating gallery walks within the school so students have the opportunity for peer critiques and compliments, we must make sure that student work is more than just a dialogue between student and teacher. When students have an authentic audience and can therefore see themselves as having an informed—if not expert—voice in the world, students will develop passion for their work. Be aware that blogging merely to blog grows old, and we must work to create real audience opportunities, rather than just counting on the somewhat overwhelming nature of a Google search to create an audience.

- Make it last. When students move from unconnected project to unconnected project, students can lose the sense of urgency and passion, but when students have the opportunity to see a project through multiple revisions, through multiple iterations, it becomes theirs. When students care enough about a project to hand it down to younger students to continue the work, you know that students have a passion for what they have created.

———— **84** ————

꙰

Teach Kindness

*Hello babies. Welcome to Earth. It's hot in the summer and cold in the
winter. It's round and wet and crowded. On the outside, babies,
you've got a hundred years here. There's only one rule that I know of,
babies—"God damn it, you've got to be kind."*
                        —*Kurt Vonnegut*, God Bless You, Mr. Rosewater

High school is not structured to teach kindness.
There is almost nothing about the traditional high school
that would encourage kids to believe that the adults value kindness. Think about it. The factory model of education that persists
in most American high schools is designed to limit meaningful
human interaction, not create it.

- Forty- to fifty-minute classes
- Students seeing up to seven or eight teachers a day
- Different sets of students in every class
- Hundred-point grading scales and class ranks that
  encourage students to compete against one another
  with focus on product, ignoring process

- No longitudinal relationships between students and teachers, so there are few opportunities, aside from extracurriculars, for teachers and students to get to know one another over time
- Little to no time for meaningful collaboration among the adults

So much of the current overarching structure of high school is fundamentally individualistic, isolating, and solipsistic. What's incredible is that most teachers went into the profession because on some fundamental level, they care about kids. And without a doubt, individual teachers in schools all over the world inspire students with their acts of kindness despite being in a system that discourages rather than encourages kindness as an institutional value.

We have to recognize that teaching kindness is more than just modeling "being nice to kids"; we have to understand that kindness is essentially the act of extending one's self in the care of another. Aristotle defined it as "helpfulness towards someone in need, not in return for anything, nor for the advantage of the helper himself, but for that of the person helped."[73] And kindness is central as a profoundly important action—virtue, even—in most of the major religious and philosophical movements from Judeo-Christianity to Islam to Buddhism to humanism. It is, therefore, a moral imperative to create environments in our high schools where kindness is powerfully modeled and taught.

What are some structures that more powerfully lend themselves to learning environments that are more kind? How do we make it easier for students to be kind to one another and easier for teachers to model kindness by being able to be kind to their students?

There is no list we could create that is exhaustive, but we want to make a start. The adults who spend their lives in schools are overwhelmingly kind people. And students are capable of profound acts of kindness. The structure of school must do more to enable, support, and enhance that.

From Theory to Practice

- Create spaces for students and teachers to know each other over time. For SLA, that's Advisory. When students and teachers have a community where people can know each other not just as students and teachers of a subject, but also as people, that is a powerful opportunity for kindness. In addition, when students are encouraged to see teachers as their advocates, it gives teachers the opportunity to model kindness.

- Create more opportunities for students to feel part of a community in their classes. For example, have students spend more time with the same groups of students, integrate science and math classes, or loop students and teachers for more than a year so that the community of learners can stay together.

- Simplify grading systems and do away with individualized class rank. Educators like Joe Bower (http://www.joebower.org/) advocate doing away with grading entirely, but there are less extreme steps schools can take. Schools can move to a 4.0 GPA without plusses and minuses so that students are less competitive about their grades. Schools can report broad categories of class rank to colleges (Top 10 percent, Top 25 percent, Top 50 percent—this is what we do at SLA). All these are ways to dial down the competitiveness of high school and allow students to become more invested in the success of all members of their community.

- Have students identify and solve real problems. Many educators are using the framework of design thinking (http://www.designthinkingforeducators.com/) to help students develop empathy as they learn how to listen in order to identify problems and seek solutions.

- Create channels for positive interactions between home and school. Schedule fifteen minutes once a month in a faculty meeting for teachers to write positive emails to students and parents about great things they have seen in the classroom so that students and parents can see that school–home communication is more than informational and punitive.
- Have shared spaces. Put tables in hallways, and make the main office community space. Don't put the principal's office in the back of the main office. Eat lunch together. And when you are together, laugh. Laugh a lot.

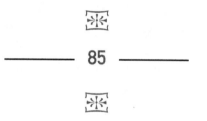

— 85 —

Make Advisory Work

The idea of Advisory is not a new one. Schools all over the country do it, but the problem is that in many schools, teachers and students will tell you that it does not function in reality as well as it could in theory. Making that switch from teachers teaching academic classes to running a community-driven classroom is a challenge that should not be underestimated. So how do we do it well? The most important thing is this: make it a priority.

In the end, the shorthand we use for thinking about how Advisory drives much of our thinking about the relationships between students and teachers can be summed up with two ideas: First, you have to think of Advisory as the soul of your school. Second, with everything you do, remember that you teach students before you teach subjects. At SLA, we believe there is a difference between saying, "I teach English" and "I teach kids English." Kids should never be the implied object of their own education. Advisory is the place in the schedule where that idea has its core; then it spreads into everything else we do.

From Theory to Practice

- Schedule Advisory with real time. Don't make that time the dumping ground or the place you steal time from whenever something else comes up. Don't make it first thing in the morning so it is easy to skip. Treat it as a real class that teachers have to prepare for, because while it may not be as much work from a grading perspective, the time and energy teachers will spend caring for children, getting to know families, and dealing with issues that come up is real. Advisory cannot be the thing teachers deal with after they have dealt with everything else, or it will just be "homeroom," as it is in so many places. For us, that means scheduling fifty minutes for Advisory at the end of the day, twice a week, and having teachers teach four classes plus Advisory instead of five classes plus homeroom as they would in other School District of Philadelphia schools.

- Don't assume that teachers know how to care for children—teach them how to. We love Carol Lieber's book *The Advisory Guide*[74] as a foundation text. Do a book study with teachers about it. Then have a subcommittee that helps to draft a framework for the curriculum, with broad themes for each year and examples of ways to execute them. Our committee includes our health teacher, our counselors, and some of the teachers who are really invested in Advisory, and they set the agenda (with school leadership) on how to run workshops for our faculty.

- Make it matter by making it a core function of the school. We don't have traditional parent-teacher conferences at SLA. We have parent-student-advisor conferences where teachers all write narrative report cards, which are then processed, talked about, or reviewed by the parent, student, and advisor together. This makes the advisor the primary link to the families, which goes a long way toward really making the power of Advisory transparent to families (and teachers). If a child gets in trouble, advisors are looped in immediately. Our college counselor works with the advisors so that they are the primary school-based adults to help students make decisions about their college process.

- Don't make it "just another class." Teachers know how to teach classes, but they may not know how to have a class that is really more like group high school survival therapy. So you have to help teachers resist the urge to create assignments that can be graded and have homework, and so on. We think of Advisory as a pressure valve for kids; if it becomes something that has a lot of homework and requires a lot of work for a grade, that defeats the purpose.

——————— 86 ———————

Teachers Should Be Readers and Learners

The same way that we must want for adults what we want for students, we must do as adults what we would like students to do, particularly reading.

In the schools we need, teachers not only encourage literacy and learning, but they participate in it themselves as well.

Every school has one teacher who can point to the filing cabinet drawer when you walk into her room. "That drawer," she will tell you, "has eighth grade in it." Pointing to the other drawers, she will explain that the lesson plans and overheads for other years are all stocked away in the event that she be moved to teach another grade the next year.

Many schools have multiple versions of this teacher. Their lessons and thinking are fixed, and they see no reason to alter that course. The high-tech version of this teacher can point to the flash drives with text files and PowerPoints archived across grade levels.

Teachers must seek and engage in reading for the same reason we want our students to read—to find new ideas, challenge old ideas, and build on what they already know.

Admittedly, given the papers that need grading, the lessons that need planning, and the resources that need creating, picking up a book about teaching is not the sexiest of out-of-school activities. Finding the right books, though, can mean finding new practices that alleviate the load of traditional teaching.

While toolkit books that preach this or that newest "best practice" can be helpful for a quick top-up when teachers are struggling to figure out how to make their next units of study interesting, they aren't the best reading. These books are the paperback romance novels of the education world. They offer quick escapes from the problems of practice and don't ask their audiences to think too much about what's happening or why.

The education books worth the time it takes to read them engage teachers in thinking about why and how they do what they do in their classrooms or other learning spaces. Like the best literature, they are complex, thought-provoking, and devoid of easy answers. Readers must also do the work. Dewey, Freire, Lawrence-Lightfoot, Holt, Delpit, Dweck, and many more present ideas about education and schools that ask us to evaluate our preconceptions and remain open to the new worlds they would have us create through our practice.

We say *reading* here intentionally. There is a difference between learning through the exploration of a book (physical or digital) and reading an article in a periodical or a piece of research. A book has been thoughtfully curated. It contains a string of thoughts related to one another and pieced together by the author or authors so as to lead you through a journey of learning that can push against the mental filing cabinets labeled, "Here's what I think about this." Yes, teachers should be learners. One specific way that learning should occur is through the study of books.

Admittedly, the time crunch already mentioned is a barrier to teacher reading in the same way that the reading and other work assigned to the typical hyperscheduled student makes it hard for them to read anything else.

If we want schools to be temples dedicated to the exchange of ideas, we must create the spaces necessary for those exchanges, and we must work constantly to access, synthesize, and consider new ideas. Reading, though not the only way to access these ideas, can be a strong gateway drug for learning.

From Theory to Practice

- Interested faculty can organize a reading group that meets regularly over a common planning period, after school, or during lunch.

- In spaces where common interest cannot be mustered, encourage teachers to turn to online spaces like Goodreads.com for communities of readers, book suggestions, and conversations about what they read.

- School leaders who understand the value of common language in building culture can ask faculties to study texts they've selected as speaking to the mission, values, and goals of a school in order for all concerned to build an understanding of the common vision of the space.

- Ten minutes of every faculty meeting could be opened up to faculty members sharing pieces of something they've read since the last time everyone got together.

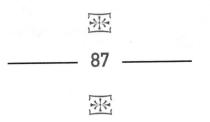

Change at School Zone Pace

As soon as they were taken up as a tent pole issues for the champions of "twenty-first-century skills," things like "research," "argumentation," and "collaborative effort" were destined to wiggle their way into the goals of any school's annual planning for at least the first two decades of the twenty-first century. By 2030, we're likely to be championing "twenty-second-century skills." For now, though, let us focus on the century at hand. Here, we'll take the implementation of collaboration as our focus, but feel free to insert your school's twenty-first-century skill of the moment. The point remains the same.

In the rush to adopt a practice of collaboration, many schools have set decrees and adopted protocols to ensure collaboration in action if not in spirit. Unless a school's culture—its leaders, its teachers, its students—has decided to own the effort of collaboration, practice by decree is sure to be mired in "almost implementation."

The schools we need allow for a school zone speed limit to taking up a practice of collaboration.

For schools having difficulties initiating new practices, the danger often lies not in doing something new or different, but in doing something much more quickly than is comfortable to those responsible for the work.

While we are firm believers in learning the work by doing the work, this does not mean doing all the work at once and expecting it to be all done well.

A school zone speed limit adoption method is similar to asking drivers to slow down when traveling through a school zone. Moving at full speed in these areas will mean they are not likely to fully appreciate what they are doing, and they will be much more liable to interfere or endanger the travels of others who are attempting to move through the same space.

These principles apply to full-speed adoption of collaboration. Asking people to jump full speed into a practice—with full integration of lesson planning, peer observation, brainstorming, curriculum planning, and so on—makes it likely that they will not notice the small but significant details along the way that are important to improving any new practices.

They will go through the motions of collaborating, just as the driver will likely still stop at a stop sign, speed zone or not. But they will not take the time—or have the time—to reflect on what happens when they change this or that element of their practice.

Slowing down, focusing on a few key elements of practice will allow those being asked for mindfulness to see and reflect on the shifting of the organization. They will be able to refine these new efforts, and the practice will evolve.

It's not always best to get somewhere as quickly as possible. To do so often means sacrificing safety and ignoring our surroundings. It's possible to move faster toward collaboration, but likely not worth it.

From Theory to Practice

- Share the work. At the top of each school-wide meeting, ask all teachers to share with those around them a single sentence explaining something they are working on with their students.
- Watch it happen. Ask for a group of teachers to volunteer to sit in on at least one of their peers' classes during a week and to welcome others to do the same in their own classes.
- Talk about it. Create a common physical or online space where teachers are asked to share questions and ideas relevant to what they are teaching or planning to teach, with immediate means for others to offer answers and suggestions.
- Talk about the work of others. Allocate five minutes at the beginning of every faculty meeting for teachers to stand and share those things they saw that they identified as good in a peer's classrooms since the previous meeting.
- The list could continue forever. Indeed, as a learning organization feels more and more comfortable with collaborative practice and begins to speed up, the list is likely to lengthen exponentially.

—————— 88 ——————

⌖

Create Space for Collaboration

As we think about evolving practice in education, we must also consider how our physical spaces must also adapt to a changing pedagogy. Collaboration, as anyone talking about the evolution of education will tell you, is a good thing. Some will argue that collaboration is a twenty-first-century skill—as though civilization would have had any chance at progressing to this point had people not been collaborating for various virtuous and nefarious purposes.

As we have stumbled upon collaboration again, perhaps we could be more purposeful in its execution.

Ask a principal if they want their teachers to be collaborating with one another, and you're likely to find that all will say "yes." You are equally likely to hear multitudinous reasons why it's not happening. Chief among these is some variation on, "Well, I've done my best to encourage collaboration among my staff, but they don't seem to want to collaborate with one another or to take the time to collaborate."

This is not surprising.

In the schools we need, we must not only encourage collaboration; we must also make space for it. Those same principals who lament the lack of faculty interest in collaboration are rarely mindful of the space they've created for such a culture shift in their schools.

Proclamation of a collaborative spirit must be accompanied by both physical and temporal space for the implementation of that spirit. To a principal it can appear that their encouragement has fallen on deaf ears. To teachers, this is often not the case. They have heard the calls for working together to design, execute, and refine new teaching practices, but they are left wondering what, if anything, they can let go of to make space for such efforts.

Without leadership and the permission to end certain practices that inhibit collaboration, principals' encouragement to begin collaborating will be heard as asking to do more with less.

To foster collaborative spaces, schools must consider redesigning schedules in ways that allow the breathing room for teachers to work together without the pressure to complete other prescribed tasks. In some cases, this will mean keeping time on the schedule clear of administrative minutiae.

If collaborative time is to be privileged within a school, then it must be prioritized clearly and without conditions in the school schedule.

Similarly, the school must designate collaborative physical spaces where teachers know they can go to sit with their peers, share ideas, and gain helpful feedback on what they are creating. These are spaces where the school's resources are aggregated, shared, and celebrated to encourage their examination and remixing by anyone interested. For some, this may sound like a school library. For others, it might be a faculty lounge. For many, it may sound like no space that yet exists at their school. For all, these should be spaces that help to serve as a physical hub of collaboration. For us at SLA, there are many spaces, but the main office is one of the most important places. Most school main offices are very compartmentalized. By creating an open office where adults and students alike can collaborate, we hope we send a powerful message about the value of collaboration.

Professing a collaborative atmosphere is one thing. Having a collaborative atmosphere requires creating actual times and spaces where collaboration can grow and spread into the culture of a school.

From Theory to Practice

- Create physical spaces for collaboration. No matter where it is, make a deliberate space whose purpose is allowing folks to work, to talk, to be together.
- Create virtual spaces for collaboration. A tool as simple and as powerful as Google Drive, with shared documents and shared folders, can transform the workflow of a school. Lesson plans, unit plans, school plans—all can and should be shared.
- Create the mind-set for collaboration. Start projects together. Create time for people to work together—common planning time, weekly faculty meetings, school committees that have the authority to work with the administration to enact real change. Collaboration works when people can see the changes it brings.

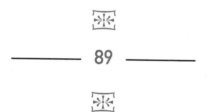

Work Together to Make Us All Better

In a room filled with teachers of students from grades 6 to 12, the discussion is focused on the new direction for the school. On the table at the moment: the question of yearly themes and grade-level essential questions.

A teacher, not convinced of the need for either, raises her hand. "Why do we need themes? Why can't we just trust that teachers will go into their classrooms, do their very best for students, and help them learn?"

The overarching constructs being debated sound a lot like further encroachment on the territory of teachers' professional judgment.

"And," the teacher added, "isn't me prescribing essential questions just more teacher-centered learning? What if these aren't the questions my students have? Why can't each student decide which questions are most interesting?" Again, the questions smack of contrivances and the undercutting of student interests.

Two responses are key to this teacher's questions. The first is general and free of considerations of the merits of her arguments. Surveying the room, every teacher, not the consultant who's been brought in to facilitate the conversation, should have an answer to this teacher's questions. Each teacher should, to varying degrees of detail, be able to proffer an answer as to why this is the way forward for their faculty and students.

Without an ability to explain why what they are proposing is what they should be doing, this faculty, like many others, will not move forward. Rather, they will move everywhere. Without a clear philosophy of practice as described by Dewey in *Experience and Education*,[75] this school (or any school) will not know why they are doing what they are doing, and they will not know whether they are doing it well.

Many contemporary schools are suffering from both mission drift and theory drift. Some began with visionary leaders and teams who possessed clear, sound arguments for why they would do what they would do in a certain way toward the goal of teaching children. Inevitably, as time passes, more urgent matters erupt, and faculty change, that initial vision can become clouded or forgotten.

The hope, for this school at least, would be that prior to ratifying any specific change of course, each member of the teaching community be asked to explain both what they want for the school and why they want it. If each teacher can do this, the future will look much brighter.

The second response is a direct answer to the questions posed. It has several parts. First, trusting teachers to do the very best they know how to do is not in question. On an individual basis, some training may be necessary and some teachers may not be up to snuff. Themes, essential questions, and other silo-breaking curricular elements mean creating pathways for teachers to do their very best together through the sharing, challenging, and iteration of ideas. Cross-classroom components build space for teachers to do better by doing together. It staves off the siloed teaching of traditional classrooms and raises new questions.

Such elements also work to eliminate the false boundaries between "subjects" established by the traditional structures of schools. By working across classes to answer a question like "What is my role in my community?" students can come to realize there isn't one answer, nor does any answer belong to a specific class or subject area. Citizenship, literacy, ethics, anything—these are themes and understandings that have implications across all areas of learning, and any question asked without considering all disciplines would be the lesser for its exclusion.

Finally, two aspects of the question of excluding student interests must be addressed. First, concerning teachers working separately and allowing students to chase the answers to their individual questions: Does every teacher at this school actually have the practical and professional capacity to help each individual student in his or her care ask whatever questions are of interest? If the answer is "yes," this school is unique in its capacity and should be captured for study. If the answer is the more likely "no," then the students would be better served and the teachers' stress greatly reduced by a team approach to drawing out curiosity and crafting experiences around it.

Second, there are issues we as educators and professionals understand more deeply than our students do. We have the "mature" knowledge, as Dewey described it, and we should not fear directing student learning in a thoughtful, goal-based way to help students become the citizens we need and intend. This rests on the assumption already mentioned: we must be intentional with our practice, and we must not be ashamed of our own expertise.

Working together need not mean sacrificing individuality. Providing for student choice does not mean abdicating a teacher's responsibility to direct. There's more complexity than an assumed dichotomy would suggest.

From Theory to Practice

- Have fewer mandates. There are many schools that move from one big idea to another, year after year, without ever building consensus on why or how those ideas are going to be implemented. Thoughtful school change involves all members having the time and space to work through an idea. Not everyone will agree all the time, but dissent should be honored.

- Brainstorm together. Sit down as a grade group and make lists of all the themes and big ideas that are touched on across the curriculum. Look for moments of commonality. Ask the big question of "How would this big idea become more powerful if students asked it across the different subject areas?"

────── 90 ──────

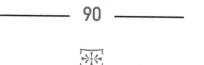

Get Together

One of the best things we do at SLA is get together. This includes our faculty meetings and the side conversations that take place there, the happy hours and birthday celebrations—and it's more than that. Those gatherings are about the faculty. The best moments of getting together are around being a school.

In the schools we need, people get together.

It starts in ninth grade. About a month into the school year, a few dedicated parents of upper classmen staff a bank of phones in the main office. They are calling other parents—the parents of the newest class of students—to invite them to the annual back-to-school (BTS) night. SLA has a BTS night, as every school across Philadelphia and across the country does, to welcome new students and parents and introduce them to the school, the adults, and the building.

But SLA's BTS night is different. While those parents are on the phone, they're not only offering an invitation, they're making a request: "Bring something to eat." SLA's BTS is also a potluck, with each new ninth-grade family invited to bring a dish, one that is pivotal to the family if possible. Gatherings are better with food.

Our first year of the tradition, Chris was worried we wouldn't have enough food. A few hundred people would gather in our cafeteria and all we'd have to offer is a cheese platter. As families started to arrive that first year, so did the food. Everyone who was hungry ate that night (including the students who'd hung around after extracurriculars).

It's not just about the eating, of course; it's the cementing of community as well. Parents, students, advisors—they all sit together, share a meal in the din of noise in a high school café-gym-atorium, and begin the get-together that will be these students' tenure in high school.

While they eat, those teachers who work with ninth-grade students circulate, introduce themselves, and briefly answer questions about what the upcoming year will hold.

Later in the evening, there are formal talks, people introducing themselves through a microphone, but this is not, nor should it be, about speeches. This is about getting together, talking, listening, and welcoming into a community.

Four years later, with many events and meetings in between, this gathering finds its bookend. The obvious guess would be that the bookend is graduation. That would be wrong. Graduation ceremonies are for the students and their families. We get together for graduation because we honor what these students have accomplished and the new journey they are beginning.

No, the bookend comes after graduation. The faculty gather together, walk a few blocks to a local restaurant, and, weather permitting, sit under the sky alongside their colleagues who each knew these students for at least a semester, and close the chapter on the work of the last four years.

For teachers, this is as much a get-together of grieving as it is of celebration. Many will never know where these students end up or what they do with their learning of the last four years. The teachers have done their job, and they are now to prepare for the next class, the next BTS night, and all the students in between. They share food, drink, and memories. Some pass around the handwritten cards from students for whom they played a key role in the last few years.

These get-togethers are as important to the teachers as they are to the students they will meet in the coming fall. It is a reminder that they have done what they were charged to do, and that it is more than a job. It is also a reminder that time will march on and that this is a profession not for martyrs, but for practitioners.

Getting together, being together, is important in the life of a school. This is different from a meeting or a happy hour. It is a kind of formative and summative reflection for a community that plants a mile marker for the organization. "We are here, now, together, and we will acknowledge it and remember where we've been." Without taking the time to get together, no group can go anywhere together.

From Theory to Practice

- Break bread. It need not be a back-to-school night, but find a way to ask your students and their families to join together and enjoy a meal. It's easy to become titles—teacher, student, guardian—and lose our humanity in one another's eyes. Zac and his coadvisor Matt Kay scheduled a separate meal later in the school year where their twenty advisees and their families came together to discuss the first year of high school and what they could expect.

- Involve everyone. If it was SLA's school secretary, Ms. Diane, or Chris on the line each year to call the new families and invite them to BTS, the tradition would likely get lost under the load of the urgent matters that crop up through the school day. Because the parents own a piece of the potluck and the teachers know they will be talking to their future students, everyone is committed to making the night a success, so continuing the tradition is less work.

- Appreciate the informal. It need not be a production. No space need be rented, no reservations made. Make the time for a happy hour after work, a field trip to a local point of interest, an exploration day where parents tour the school while it's in operation. Whatever the effort, appreciate that getting together is about time spent together rather than how much you planned for that time.

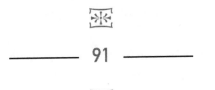

—— 91 ——

We Must Practice a New Kind of Research

Time was that you knew what research meant when a teacher announced to the class that they'd be conducting it. The library would be reserved (God only knows what would happen if more than one group of students was in there at once). The librarian could be counted upon to deliver the perfunctory "Here's How We Use the Library" speech. And the class would be released to find the handful of books related to their respective topics.

For those in high school who took an old-school approach, research also meant a plethora of note cards—source cards, quote cards, outline cards. Cards galore. It was a simpler time, a calmer time, and, quite frankly, a better time for note card manufacturers.

Say "research" now, and a myriad of scenarios runs through students' and teachers' heads. Maybe a library is involved. Maybe they turn to their phones. Maybe it's a computer lab or laptop cart; perhaps both. If it's the latter, an Internet connection is handy, but the options only open up from there. Will students use the simplified pay-for-use services? Will they Google? Will they plagiarize? Will the teacher catch on?

The possibilities are endless. Research is different now, and the schools we need see research questions as both "what?" and "how?"

To accomplish this, we must work to make sure teachers know how to find felicitous answers in any landscape. This doesn't mean another seminar on how to use the latest subscription database. Helping schools be centers of research means helping teachers develop the habits of practice that help them to make informed and efficient decisions in an information landscape. When we do this, teachers can then more powerfully help students because, in the end, teachers who have a love for and understanding of research will pass this on to students.

And as always, teacher work should be driven by the same things we hope for students—inquiry and projects worth completing. At SLA, teachers have engaged in research in pedagogical practice in the classroom, larger questions about education and American society, and the question of school-wide reform as we have worked to become better as an institution.

To this end, schools working to become learning organizations are asking questions. Their teachers have ideas and questions as to what needs to be done to improve teaching and learning in the space, and they are asked to do generative work that moves practices forward.

It stands to reason that teachers who are active researchers themselves are much more likely to be better teachers of researchers.

Students presented with the staid practices of note card–based research or any derivatives thereof are likely to notice (and rightly so) that these strategies ask them to devolve what are likely highly complex methods for tracking down information.

Instead, we must realize we are beyond being beholden to what can be found from a single source. Hypertextual sources mean students can track from one source to another to another, ad infinitum. Anyone who's jumped down the rabbit hole of Wikipedia knows this to be true.

The "how?" and "what?" questions are ever more important.

In helping students to be researchers, teachers must pose and invite inquiry around some key questions:

What information is relevant to what I want to know?
What information is irrelevant to what I want to know?
How will I know the difference?
What kinds of places might hold interesting knowledge about
    my questions?
Whom might I want to access to better understand my interests?

Some key components of these questions should jump out immediately. In a super-informed space, it isn't only about what information can be found; it is important to consider which information is both relevant as well as interesting. When we were counting on the five books from the library, we didn't need to discern between what was interesting and what wasn't. It was a seller's market, and we took notes on every mundane fact we could find to be able to reach our page requirement.

Contemporary researchers are flush with relevant and irrelevant as well as interesting and uninteresting information. Teaching how to make the distinction is key.

Books also held us to their author's page-contained views on a topic or a journalist's one-off article on an event. Contemporary researchers have more ready access to people as well as ideas. In asking whom they might want to contact, students are more likely to consider how they might leverage social technologies to communicate with sources in real time. Drawing on sources from email to Twitter, students can publish a report Friday that includes information from an interview Wednesday.

Doing research today must be about asking better questions with respect to the "how?" of the questions we're asking. It must also allow teachers to practice the kinds of information-gathering and synthesis they're asking of students. In such an ecosystem we are driven not only to ask complex questions, but to craft complex answers as well.

From Theory to Practice

- Create the space for teacher inquiry groups. Let teachers choose topics related to their passion and their profession, and encourage the modern research practices that move beyond the note cards for teachers as well.

- Share research. Create space—digital and analog—where teachers' action research can live. Make pathways for peer review so that good ideas can spread. Use research to influence school-wide and classroom practice. Invite local schools of education to have student teachers and professors join that space, so that preservice teachers can see current practitioners engage in research as a model.

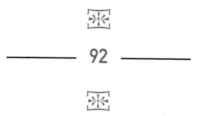

Experts Are Necessary

In a conference panel presentation on the crafting of public policy, the floor is opened to questions from the audience.

Throughout the conversation, mention has been made of how new technologies have opened up pathways for dialogue between policymakers and citizens toward the goal of a more democratic society.

In this vein, an audience member steps up to the microphone and suggests the possibility of crowdsourcing a policy on something like telecommunications or open government. "Wouldn't something like this be the ultimate in democracy?" he asks.

It is a fair question, given the direction of the conversation up to this point. The answer, though, is better than the question. It is a stark reminder that, despite the proliferation of information, some of us know things other people don't.

"I'm not sure how that would work," one of the panelists responds, "and I think it's a good idea to remember there are experts on these topics who understand the nuance of these issues." She points to two fellow panelists who have worked at the highest levels of city and federal government. "I'm glad that we have people like these to whom we can turn for these complex issues."

In the schools we need, it's important to remember experts are acceptable.

The most obvious application of this principle is to the role of teachers. In an instant-info-saturated age, it is tempting to suggest the death of the expert. When anything from auto repair to ordination can be found within seconds, the role of the teacher could appear to be hazy. In truth, it has never been more important to bring precision to what we see as the place of the teacher in learning spaces. Those who have paid lip service to their roles as "facilitators of learning" and "helping students on journeys of discovery" while retaining teaching practices that feature long lectures and worksheets will be forced to decide whether they pass their own muster.

John Dewey maintained the need for an authority in children's lives who helped guide them in finding questions worth asking and materials worth using. Learners need experts.

Dewey's other major goal for education—the crafting of educational experiences—is also more within reach than ever before. Tools and connectivity mean students can take on roles as junior experts in areas they find interesting without committing to a full journeyman model that has them apprenticing for nearly a decade to vocations that they're interested in only as hobbies.

Here too, experts are valuable. They offer a bar for comparison as students mess about in learning experiences. These bars help students remember they are not experts after completing what David Perkins refers to as the "junior varsity version of the game."[76] Yes, they've gained understanding and ability after participating in the acquisition and synthesis of knowledge, but there's always more work to be done, and there's always someone to learn from.

Experts are valuable in the sense that the panelist pointed out in response to the questioner in the preceding conference scenario. They help us to navigate some of the more complex nuances of the issues and problems we try to solve. In the classroom, they can help us find the right questions to ask and to organize learning experiences. Perhaps most important, experts help us to understand what we don't know in a straightforward sense and as a basis for comparison in our own development. The schools we need see and appreciate each of these expert spaces, and the adults and children in these schools know when to turn to experts as they work to turn into experts.

From Theory to Practice

- Trust your gut, and confirm with research. The U.S. Department of Education's What Works Clearinghouse (http://ies.ed.gov/ncee/wwc/) aims to pull together the best research in education sciences and make it easily accessible to practitioners in the field. If you've got a good idea for a change in your school, it's likely there's compelling research to back it up. Searching places like the Clearinghouse can add nuance and shape to your instincts and help prevent missteps already made by others.

- Experts need not be academics. Similar to the policy experts in the conference example, students come with their own experts—their families. The adults and other folks who have helped get your students to the point that they're ready for your school and classroom can speak to your ideas for new approaches to making content accessible better than anyone else in their lives (save the students themselves).

- Determine the details. If your students are coming to school hungry, you could go the path of teacher martyrdom and spend your own money on feeding them. Sometimes this may be the only way. Many times, though, cities and towns have programs to help put food in the stomachs of hungry students, taking advantage of resources of which you may be unaware. Connecting with human services experts in your area can help serve students and families in systemic ways.

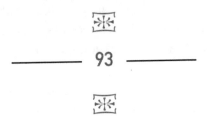

—— 93 ——

Success Must Be Defined by All

The setting is a familiar one. A teacher sits across the table from an administrator. Both have note-taking devices in front of them. The teacher's—a spiral notebook and a pen he found on the floor after his last class. The administrator's—an iPad with stylus.

They begin their debrief of the lesson the administrator has just observed. She pulls up the lesson plan the teacher submitted the day before using the district-approved template.

"I noticed the learning objective wasn't on the board," the administrator begins after some small talk.

And we're off to the races.

While several pieces of the above scenario are glaringly unsettling, the piece to be focused on is not even mentioned.

In the schools we need, the adults must be working from a common and cocreated definition of success.

When teachers and administrators sit down to debrief, they are not likely to have a conversation about what a successful lesson looks like through each other's eyes.

Any debrief conversation is likely to sound much like each person talking about an element they saw as successful (or not), and the other responding by attempting to fit that element into their own definition or argue against its importance.

A favorite question to ask school and district leaders at the top of any school year is, "What are three things you would like to achieve in order to count your school or district as successful this year?"

For most, such a frank and open question is met with a long nonanswer that ends with "all children being successful." If we're really lucky, they'll also throw in "lifelong learners."

Learning spaces that engage in conversations about their definitions of success are doing more than setting goals; they are setting culture as well. As Harvard Graduate School of Education Research Professor Richard Elmore says, "Language is culture."[77]

By defining success together, administrators and teachers sidestep a language imbalance wherein discussions of teaching and learning are loaded with the language of administrators and result in teachers attempting to translate what they do into that language. Such unequal conversations are classroom-level instances of educational colonialism in which the teachers are the colonized.

Instead, imagine a meeting at the close of a school year where all of the adults in the school sit together and are asked to write their responses to two questions:

Were we successful this year?

What makes you say that?

Two simple questions with the ability to uncover great swaths of unspoken cultural beliefs of the organization.

Move forward to the reconvening of the school the next fall. Rather than standing in front of those assembled and speaking to them as though the year ahead and the people it will include are wholly separate from the previous school year, the principal returns to the questions with which the school concluded the last year.

"Here is how we defined success last year," she says, distributing a listing of people's anonymous responses grouped by similarities. "The question we must decide moving forward is 'How will we, as a learning organization, decide to define success this year?'"

From there, the hard work begins: moving from a group of adults tacitly assuming they're working toward the same measures of success to explicitly stating the standard toward which they will be working that year. Uncovering assumptions is a difficult and sometimes painful task. It may result in some teachers realizing their visions of success do not align with the goals of the school and asking them if they are willing to realign their definitions or if it is time for them to find another community better-synced with their beliefs.

The difference lies in the cocreation of success and the ownership by all adults of the definition of that success.

Returning to our teacher and administrator debrief, imagine the conversation they would be able to have and the language they would share as a result of a shared definition of success. Imagine, then, teachers having the freedom to have the same conversations with their students.

Imagine the democracy of such a school.

From Theory to Practice

- Stop reinventing the wheel every year. Goals should evolve, but 90-degree shifts—or worse, 180-degree shifts—are jarring to students and teachers alike, and more often than not are due to administrative edicts as opposed to a democratically developed process.

- Be reflective about success. Create spaces throughout the year for teachers to be honest and reflective about their progress through the year. Make these moments formative, not summative, so that teachers will be honest.

- Share goal-setting. Come together as a faculty and define school-wide goals that can help inform personal goals. Often, individual goals do not connect to the larger vision of the school because that larger vision has not been spelled out. One way to encourage a faculty to grow together as a unit is to share school-wide goals that then help inform personal goals.

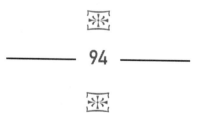

—————— 94 ——————

We Don't Need Martyrs

We need no martyrs here.

It's easy, in the conversation about education, to point to the martyrs. The system is set up to invite martyrdom.

"Do more with less," say states, districts, and principals (outright or otherwise). "Teach these students with books from two decades ago, no classroom supplies, and a drive toward academic standards but a neglect of standards of humanity."

Structurally, teaching looks like it should be a breeding ground for martyrs.

As contracts around the country are calling for extended days without additional pay, value-added models include values not directly in teachers' control, and communities are asking schools to do much more than imprinting the three Rs, it is little wonder martyrdom is a main characteristic of a teacher's prep period.

The teaching load is getting heavier, class sizes are expanding, and the mission is more complicated.

Teachers have every reason to complain about pay, workload, and the demands of the job.

But there's a difference between complaining and protesting, and martyring ourselves. The most important difference? We don't need another martyr. Teaching doesn't need another person who steps away from education and says, "I gave everything I had to that school and those kids, and I just can't do it anymore."

We also don't need another story of "nice white lady" syndrome where the fresh-faced teacher walks into the class of marginalized students. She's determined to make a difference no matter the odds or the cost to her personal life.

Teaching isn't an all-or-nothing proposition, and we are building an unsustainable system each time we perpetuate the idea that it is.

You are not the savior of students. You are not the one they have been waiting for. No prophecy has foretold your coming. You are a person of passion and training who is working to help other people learn. That is good, and it should be enough. You are helping. You are the shoulder on which to cry. You are the one who connects your students with the resources they desperately need. You will not be the one who "saves" them. To suggest as much robs students of their resiliency and agency. It assumes your world is better or worth more than their own. It assumes a lot, and ignores many important questions. Millions of students who have survived horrible existences have made it through without you. You can help, but they are not waiting for you.

The first step to moving away from a martyr mind-set in education is remembering you're not the only one.

If you weren't in your classroom, someone else would be. They wouldn't approach things the same way you do. They wouldn't have the same inside jokes with students, and they wouldn't challenge authority with the same vigor, to be sure. Still, someone would be in there, and their time is just as valuable as yours. If you think you are God's gift to teaching, you haven't been teaching long enough.

Also, if it costs you everything, it's costing you too much.

If the second largest drain on your paycheck is supplies for your students, if your personal relationships outside of school are suffering because you can't talk about anything other than your students, if you have to get a second job to support your teaching, then you're doing it wrong.

Teachers deserve a fair wage. They should be able to teach and support themselves without worrying whether they're going to make the rent. To accept anything less as a teacher is to contribute to the deprofessionalization of the practice. Accepting a position teaching for anything less than a living wage hurts us all. It makes teaching seem expendable, it discounts the investments we've made in our own learning, and it tells schools we're willing to settle. We aren't. If a school or district isn't willing to pay what you need, go somewhere else (and know that somewhere else might be many miles away.)

Teaching is an amazing profession. It affords adults a window into and a hand in the construction of discovery and learning like few others. It is a noble and necessary profession that requires the most caring, prepared, intellectual people it can find. It is not, nor should it ever be, a place for martyrs or those looking to carry a cross.

Anyone who stands in a classroom (of whatever sort) is to be honored by the surrounding community. This person deserves respect, a fair wage, and access to the resources necessary to making our schools temples of discovery and learning. Those temples, though, must not require anyone to bear a cross.

From Theory to Practice

- Take care of yourself. Create spaces for yourself to be outside of work. Whether that is by joining a neighborhood non-educational book club, playing Ultimate Frisbee, coaching your kids' swim team, or just making sure that every Saturday night is date night with your partner, hold it as sacrosanct. Every teacher deserves space for their own joy. Don't even think of it as the thing you do that replenishes you for teaching. It is not. It is the thing you do for your own joy.

- Communicate. One way out of the martyr complex is to work with others. Find time to talk to the other teachers in your building about what you are thinking. Take part in any of the dozens of Twitter chats about education. There is incredible work being done every day all over the world by millions of teachers. Understanding that you are one of many is a powerful way to short-circuit that feeling of being "the one."

- Listen to your students. Create the time to go to lunch with students and sit and listen to them in their off-times. Much of the structure of school is set up to encourage the "savior" teacher mentality, so teachers need to find spaces to see themselves as part of their students' lives, but not essential to their students' lives.

—————— 95 ——————

Teachers Are Lucky

What follows is a typical day for Chris.

At 6:30 this morning, he is on a field with eighteen young men, practicing a sport they love.

At 9:00 this morning, he watches a group of students work with a teacher on a robot they are building.

At lunch, he sits with a student and her advisor and looks over financial aid packages from the various colleges she was accepted to.

And in the afternoon, he watches a group of kids performing Shakespeare in an eleventh-grade English class.

In between those events, there are emails answered, phone calls made, a memo or two written, but more important, there are lots of conversations with students and teachers—some light and fun, some serious.

We need to understand how precious that really is.

Most people don't have the kind of days teachers have. Most people don't have a chance to pull a student aside and make them think or care or wonder. Most people don't laugh as much during the days as we do. Most people don't cry as often as teachers do. Most people simply don't feel as much as we do.

And many people have to sit in offices all day long, which we have both done for a few years. School is more fun. By a lot.

This isn't to say the job is easy; it's not. The point isn't that we get our summers off or anything like that. Teachers work hard at an incredibly emotionally and intellectually challenging job every day. But we need to remember a few things:

1. No one made us do this.
2. We don't have to keep doing it.
3. We aren't the only people in the world who work hard.
4. We get to hang out with kids all day long.

We need to keep these things in perspective, because we do no one any good when we perceive ourselves to be victims or martyrs. We need to own that we made the decision to teach and to keep teaching. And it was a good decision to make, because as hard as we work, and as ridiculous as some of the policies being imposed on schools are, and as much work as we have to do, moving from theory to practice, we stay the lucky ones.

We get to teach.

Notes

1. Accessed November 29, 2013, http://www.wolframalpha.com/input/?i= Number+of+K–12+students+in+the+US—Searched. Wolfram Alpha search: Number of K–12 students in the US.
2. Accessed November 29, 2013, http://www.wolframalpha.com/input/?i= Number+of+teachers+in+the+US—Searched. – Wolfram Alpha search: Number of teachers in the US.
3. Alex Alvarez, "Rahm Emanuel to TV Interviewer: 'You Are Wrong and a Bully… I Don't Care about You,' *Mediaite*, July 22, 2011, accessed August 9, 2014, http://www.mediaite.com/tv/rahm-emanuel-to-tv-inter viewer-%E2%80%98you-are-wrong-and-a-bully%E2%80%A6-i-don%E2 %80%99t-care-about-you%E2%80%99/.
4. http://collegecostestimate.ais.psu.edu/. Penn State Help for College Cost Calculator.
5. http://www.salon.com/2011/08/29/confessions_of_a_bad_teacher/. John Owens, *Salon*, "Confessions of a Bad Teacher," August 29, 2011.
6. Science Leadership Academy, "Mission and Vision," 2010, accessed August 9, 2014, https://www.scienceleadership.org/pages/Mission_and_ Vision.
7. Relay GSE, "Our Mission and Vision," 2013, accessed August 9, 2014, http://www.relay.edu/mission/.
8. Doug Lemov, *Teach Like a Champion* (San Francisco: Jossey-Bass, 2010).
9. U.S. Department of Education, "Teacher Trends—Fast Facts," 2004, accessed August 9, 2014, http://nces.ed.gov/fastfacts/display.asp?id=28.
10. National School Reform Faculty, "Protocols A-Z," 2014, accessed August 9, 2014, http://www.nsrfharmony.org/free-resources/protocols/a-z.
11. Moveon.org, "Community Power Map Guide," 2012, accessed August 9, 2014, http://www.moveon.org/organize/campaigns/powermap.html.

12. Accessed August 7, 2014, https://sites.google.com/a/scienceleadership.org/capstone/.
13. Wikipedia, "Keeping the Faith (song)," accessed August 9, 2014, http://en.wikipedia.org/wiki/Keeping_the_Faith_(song).
14. High Tech High, http://www.hightechhigh.org/.
15. The Met Center, http://metcenter.org/.
16. Kurt Vonnegut, *Mother Night* (New York: Harper & Row, 1966, p. v).
17. Norma González, Luis C. Moll, and Cathy Amanti, eds., *Funds of Knowledge: Theorizing Practices in Households, Communities, and Classrooms* (Routledge, 2013).
18. Keynote by Michael Moe, attended by Chris Lehmann.
19. Bruce R. Joyce and Beverly Showers, *Student Achievement through Staff Development* (New York: ASCD, 2002).
20. Don McCormick and Michael Kahn, "Barn Raising: Collaborative Group Process in Seminars," *EXCHANGE: The Organizational Behavior Teaching Journal* 7.4 (1987): 16–20.
21. Alaya White, Capstone presentation, June 2011.
22. Herbert R. Kohl, *I Won't Learn from You* (New York: New Press, 1994).
23. Scott G. Paris and Julianne C. Turner, "Situated Motivation," *Student Motivation, Cognition, and Learning* (1994): 213–237.
24. John Dewey, *Experience and Education* (New York: Simon and Schuster, 2007).
25. Stuart L. Brown, *Play: How It Shapes the Brain, Opens the Imagination, and Invigorates the Soul* (New York: Penguin, 2009).
26. David Sobel, "Place-Based Education: Connecting Classroom and Community," *Nature and Listening* 4 (2004).
27. Darren Kuropatwa, "A Difference," 2005, accessed August 9, 2014, http://adifference.blogspot.com/.
28. George Lakey, *Facilitating Group Learning: Strategies for Success with Adult Learners* (Hoboken, NJ: Wiley, 2010).
29. Gordon Willard Allport, *The Nature of Prejudice* (Reading, MA: Basic Books, 1979).
30. Bruce W. Tuckman, "Developmental Sequence in Small Groups," *Psychological Bulletin* 63.6 (1965): 384.
31. Cherie Kerr, *"When I Say This … ," "Do You Mean That?"* (Santa Ana, CA: ExecuProv Press, 1998).
32. "Dan Meyer: Math Class Needs a Makeover," 2014, accessed August 9, 2014, https://www.ted.com/talks/dan_meyer_math_curriculum_makeover.
33. Patricia L. Stock, *The Dialogic Curriculum: Teaching and Learning in a Multicultural Society* (Portsmouth, NH: Boynton/Cook Publishers, 1995).
34. Melinda Anderson, "How Long Will We Tolerate Racial Profiling in Our Schools?," *Good*, accessed September 21, 2014, http://www.good.is/posts/how-long-will-we-tolerate-racial-profiling-in-our-schools.

35. Tamar Lewin, "Black Students Face More Harsh Discipline, Data Shows," *New York Times*, March 6, 2012, accessed September 21, 2014, http://www.nytimes.com/2012/03/06/education/black-students-face-more -harsh-discipline-data-shows.html.

36. Anne Henderson, Karen Mapp, *Beyond the Bake Sale* (New York: New Press, 2007).

37. Cheri J. Pascoe, *Dude, You're a Fag: Masculinity and Sexuality in High School*, with a new preface (Berkeley, CA: University of California Press, 2011).

38. Gay, Lesbian & Straight Education Network (GLSEN), "2011 National School Climate Survey," 2013, accessed August 9, 2014, http://glsen .org/nscs.

39. Robert Fulghum, *Maybe (Maybe Not)* (New York: Random House, 1995).

40. Harper Lee, *To Kill a Mockingbird* (New York: Random House, 2010).

41. Robert Pirsig, *Zen and the Art of Motorcycle Maintenance* (New York: William Morrow, 1974).

42. Jay McTighe and Grant P. Wiggins, *Essential Questions: Opening Doors to Student Understanding* (Alexandria, VA: ASCD, 2013).

43. Kurt Vonnegut, *Bagombo Snuff Box* (New York: G. P. Putnam and Sons, 1999).

44. Gary Stager, personal conversation with the author.

45. "Conrad Wolfram: Teaching Kids Real Math with Computers," 2014, accessed August 10, 2014, https://www.ted.com/talks/conrad_wolfram _teaching_kids_real_math_with_computers.

46. Alexandra Zavis and Tony Barboza, "Teacher's Suicide Shocks School," *Los Angeles Times*, 2010, accessed August 10, 2014, http://articles .latimes.com/2010/sep/28/local/la-me-south-gate-teacher-20100928.

47. "Institute for Democratic Education in America: IDEA," 2006, accessed August 10, 2014, http://www.democraticeducation.org/.

48. Science Leadership Academy, "Individualized Learning," 2010, accessed August 10, 2014, https://www.scienceleadership.org/pages/Individualized _Learning.

49. "RSA Animate—Changing Education Paradigms," 2010, accessed September 21, 2014, http://www.youtube.com/watch?v=zDZFcDGpL4U.

50. Chris Lehmann, "Complex, Not Complicated," *Practical Theory: A View from the Schoolhouse* (blog), June 23, 2013, http://practicaltheory.org/blog/ 2013/06/23/complex-not-complicated/.

51. Hal Urban, *Positive Words, Powerful Results: Simple Ways to Honor, Affirm, and Celebrate Life* (New York: Simon and Schuster, 2004).

52. "'Learning Grounds' Episode Featuring Jolon McNeil," 2013, accessed August 10, 2014 http://www.autodizactic.com/63365-more-on-the-learning-grounds-episode-featuring-jolon-mcneil/.

53. Nel Noddings, *The Challenge to Care in Schools: An Alternative Approach to Education* (2nd ed.) (New York: Teachers College Press, 2005).

54. Indra Nooyi, "The Best Advice I Ever Got," 2014, accessed August 10, 2014, http://archive.fortune.com/galleries/2008/fortune/0804/gallery.best advice.fortune/7.html.

55. "New Jersey High School Learns the ABCs of Blogging," *The Journal*, 2005, accessed August 10, 2014, http://thejournal.com/articles/2005/06/01/new-jersey-high-school-learns-the-abcs-of-blogging.aspx.

56. Jean Lave and Etienne Wenger, *Situated Learning: Legitimate Peripheral Participation* (Cambridge, UK: Cambridge University Press, 1991).

57. Jeffrey Sommers, "Behind the Paper: Using the Student-Teacher Memo," *College Composition and Communication* (1988): 77–80.

58. Pew Research Center, "Internet, Science & Tech," 2013, accessed August 10, 2014, http://www.pewinternet.org/.

59. Reenay Rogers and Vivian Wright, "Assessing Technology's Role in Communication between Parents and Middle Schools," *Electronic Journal for the Integration of Technology in Education* 7 (2008): 36–58.

60. comScore, *US Digital Year in Review 2010: A Recap of the Year in Digital Media* (February 2011).

61. Anne Henderson and Karen L. Mapp, *A New Wave of Evidence: The Impact of School, Family, and Community Connections on Student Achievement: Annual Synthesis 2002*, National Center for Family & Community Connections with Schools (2002).

62. "A Digital Bridge to Homebound Students" http://www.ascd.org/publications/educational-leadership/dec09/vol67/num04/A-Digital-Bridge-to-Homebound-Students.aspx.

63. We first heard this metaphor used by Gregg Betheil of the New York City Department of Education; we have extended it a bit.

64. Gary Stager, panel discussion at EduCon 2.0, January 2008.

65. U.S. Department of Commerce, Economics & Statistics Administration, "Exploring the Digital Nation—Computer and Internet Use at Home," November 8, 2011, accessed August 10, 2014, http://www.esa.doc.gov/Reports/exploring-digital-nation-computer-and-internet-use-home.

66. David Perkins, *Making Learning Whole: How Seven Principles of Teaching can Transform Education* (Hoboken, NJ: Wiley, 2010).

67. http://www.ed.gov/policy/gen/guid/fpco/ferpa/index.html.

68. http://www.ftc.gov/enforcement/rules/rulemaking-regulatory-reform-proceedings/childrens-online-privacy-protection-rule.

69. http://www.providencestudentunion.org/.

70. http://www.washingtonpost.com/blogs/answer-sheet/wp/2013/03/19/sixty-percent-of-adults-who-took-standardized-test-bombed/.

71. "Twitter / plugusin: @chrislehmann: Learning only..," 2013, accessed August 10, 2014, https://twitter.com/plugusin/status/318394936233951232.

72. Paraphrased from Alvin Toffler, *Future Shock* (New York: Random House, 1970, p. 275).

73. *The Rhetoric of Aristotle: An Expanded Translation with Supplementary Examples for Students of Composition and Public Speaking* (New York: Appleton, 1932).

74. Carol Leiber, *The Advisory Guide: Designing and Implementing Effective Advisory Programs in Secondary Schools* (Cambridge, MA: Educators for Social Responsibility, 2004).

75. John Dewey, *Experience and Education* (New York: Simon and Schuster, 2007).

76. Perkins, *Making Learning Whole*.

77. Author conversation with Richard Elmore.

Works Cited

"AI, Robotics, and the Future of Jobs." *Pew Research Centers Internet American Life Project RSS*. Web. August 10, 2014. <http://www.pewinternet.org/>.

Brown, Stuart L., and Christopher C. Vaughan. *Play: How It Shapes the Brain, Opens the Imagination, and Invigorates the Soul*. New York: Avery, 2009. Print.

Christensen, Clayton M., Michael B. Horn, and Curtis W. Johnson. *Disrupting Class: How Disruptive Innovation Will Change the Way the World Learns*. New York: McGraw-Hill, 2008. Print.

Delpit, Lisa D. *Other People's Children: Cultural Conflict in the Classroom*. New York: New Press, 1996. Print.

Dewey, John. *Experience and Education*. New York: Macmillan, 1938. Print.

"Fortune." *The Best Advice I Ever Got*. August 10, 2014. <http://archive.fortune.com/galleries/2008/fortune/0804/gallery.bestadvice.fortune/7.html>.

Goldstein, Dana. *The Teacher Wars: A History of America's Most Embattled Profession*. Doubleday, 2014.

Henderson, Anne T. *Beyond the Bake Sale: The Essential Guide to Family-School Partnerships*. New York: New Press, 2007. Print.

Joyce, Bruce R., and Beverly Showers. *Student Achievement through Staff Development*. New York: Longman, 1988. Print.

Kerr, Cherie, and Julia Sweeney. *"When I Say This ... ," "Do You Mean That?": Enhancing On-the-Job Communication Skills Using the Rules and the Tools of the Improv Comedy Player*. Santa Ana, CA: ExecuProv, 1998. Print.

Kohl, Herbert R. *I Won't Learn from You: And Other Thoughts on Creative Maladjustment*. New York: New Press, 1994. Print.

Lakey, George. *Facilitating Group Learning: Strategies for Success with Diverse Adult Learners*. San Francisco: Jossey-Bass, 2010. Print.

Lave, Jean, and Etienne Wenger. *Situated Learning: Legitimate Peripheral Participation*. Cambridge: Cambridge UP, 1991. Print.

Lee, Harper. *To Kill a Mockingbird*. Philadelphia: Lippincott, 1960. Print.

Lortie, Dan C. *Schoolteacher: A Sociological Study*. Chicago: Univ. Chicago P, 1975. Print.

Los Angeles Times. "Teacher's Suicide Shocks School." September 28, 2010. <http://articles.latimes.com/2010/sep/28/local/la-me-south-gate-teacher-20100928>.

McKeachie, Wilbert James, Paul R. Pintrich, Donald R. Brown, and Claire E. Weinstein. *Student Motivation, Cognition, and Learning: Essays in Honor of Wilbert J. McKeachie*. Hillsdale, NJ: Erlbaum, 1994. Print.

McTighe, Jay, and Grant P. Wiggins. *Essential Questions: Opening Doors to Student Understanding*. Print.

Mccormick, D., and M. Kahn. "Barn Raising: Collaborative Group Process in Seminars." *Journal of Management Education* 7.4 (1982): 16–20. Print.

"National School Climate Survey." Gay, Lesbian & Straight Education Network (GLSEN). Web. August 9, 2014. <http://glsen.org/nscs>.

"New Jersey High School Learns the ABCs of Blogging." *The Journal*. Web. August 10, 2014. <http://thejournal.com/articles/2005/06/01/new-jersey-high-school-learns-the-abcs-of-blogging.aspx>.

Noddings, Nel. *The Challenge to Care in Schools: An Alternative Approach to Education*. New York: Teachers College, 1992. Print.

Pascoe, C. J. *Dude, You're a Fag: Masculinity and Sexuality in High School*. Berkeley: Univ. California P, 2007. Print.

Perkins, David N. *Making Learning Whole: How Seven Principles of Teaching Can Transform Education*. San Francisco: Jossey-Bass, 2009. Print.

Pirsig, Robert M. *Zen and the Art of Motorcycle Maintenance: An Inquiry into Values*. New York: Morrow, 1974. Print.

Poliner, Rachel A., and Carol Miller Lieber. *The Advisory Guide: Designing and Implementing Effective Advisory Programs in Secondary Schools*. Cambridge, MA: Educators for Social Responsibility, 2004. Print.

Rose, Mike. *Why School?: Reclaiming Education for All of Us*. New York: New Press, 2009. Print.

Schlosser, Eric. *Fast Food Nation: The Dark Side of the All-American Meal*. Boston: Houghton Mifflin, 2001. Print.

Sobel, David. *Place-Based Education: Connecting Classrooms & Communities*. Great Barrington, MA: Orion Society, 2005. Print.

Stock, Patricia L. *The Dialogic Curriculum: Teaching and Learning in a Multicultural Society*. Portsmouth, NH: Boynton/Cook, 1995. Print.

Toffler, Alvin. *Future Shock*. New York: Random House, 1970. Print.

Tyack, David B., and Larry Cuban. *Tinkering toward Utopia: A Century of Public School Reform*. Cambridge, MA: Harvard UP, 1995. Print.

Vonnegut, Kurt. *Bagombo Snuff Box: Uncollected Short Fiction*. New York: Putnam, 1999. Print.

Vonnegut, Kurt. *God Bless You, Mr. Rosewater: Or, Pearls before Swine*. New York: Delacorte, 1965. Print.

Vonnegut, Kurt. *Mother Night*. New York: Delacorte, 1966. Print.

Wiggins, Grant P., and Jay McTighe. *Understanding by Design*. Alexandria, VA: Association for Supervision and Curriculum Development, 1998. Print.

Index